WIFE AFTER DEATH

This book is dedicated to my husband, Bob

love without reservation

1941-1982

WIFE AFTER DEATH

WOMEN
COPING AND GROWING
AFTER THE DEATH OF A PARTNER

M. L. Anderson

Fitzhenry & Whiteside

Markham, Ontario

1993

WIFE AFTER DEATH

Fitzhenry & Whiteside
195 Allstate Parkway
Markham, Ontario L3R 4T8

Canadian Cataloguing in Publication Data

Anderson, M. L. (Margaret Lynn)
  Wife after death : women coping and growing after
the death of a partner

2nd ed.
Includes bibliographical references.
ISBN 1-55041-111-X

1. Widows — Psychology. 2. Grief. 3. Bereavement —
Psychological aspects. 4. Death — Psychological
aspects. 1. Title.

BF575.G7A63 1994   155.9'37   C93-094775-4

Typeset by Video Text Inc., Barrie, Ont.
        Jay Tee Graphics Ltd., Richmond Hill, Ont.
Printed and bound: Metropole Litho Inc.

Also by the same author:
*Alone and Growing: How to run a grief work support group for
widowed persons*

I want to acknowledge the love, support and good humour of:

my children, Jeff, Cathy, Matt and Sarah
my family
my women friends
my men friends
my Shalom friends
my neighbourhood friends
my "Alone and Growing" group friends
my poet and friend, Joanne Miller
my photographer, Les Ste. Marie
my cover designer and father, Jim McGorman
my publishing mentors, Paul and Silvio
my editors Cathy, Jane and Joanne
my typist, Joan Nickle

and

the many widowed women
without whose love and loss
this work could not have been.

Table of Contents

Author's Note

There are a lot of us, wives after death. We are looking for something. Because we have experienced the end of life we need to grieve. But more, we need to know "Why death?" And then we need to say "Hello life" while we still have it

Ultimately we all crave fulfillment and wholeness. It is the aim of this book to help widowed women find what they seek.

Chapter Outline

CHAPTER	SITUATION*	CONTENT
PEGGY	Car Accident 1982 38 4 Teacher	*Wife or Widow* Identity Crisis: Admitting What You Are
BETTY	Emphysema 1971 68 1 Business: Retired	*Trust Restored* Death, Loss and Faith
LOUISE	Tornado Victim 1974 41 3 Nurse	*Needing Others* Social Isolation and Beginning a Support Group
DEBBY	Suicide 1981 33 3 Receptionist	*Healing Oneself* Suicide and Journal Writing
JANE	Cancer 1980 43 2 Public Relations	*The Empty Nest* After the Children Go and Professional Counselling

---

* Cause of husband's death; Year of husband's death; Age then; Number of children; Training.

CHAPTER OUTLINE

SYLVIA

Cancer
1947 29 1
1983 67 2
Musicologist

The Danger Zone
Remarriage: Losing
and Gaining Oneself

HELEN

Heart Surgery
Pull Life Support
1982 39 1
Business
Administrator

Needing a Man
Dating and
Overcoming the Fear

Foreword

I met Peggy Anderson in 1985 at a retreat. It was a blustery November and the old schoolhouse was jammed with people. Overwhelmed by the emotional atmosphere, we quickly found each other as soul mates and said "Let's get out of here and go for a walk." We spent the next three days talking to each other. I knew I'd come across a remarkable woman and didn't want to let go when the session was finished. We became friends.

Peggy told me about an idea she had for a book about widows: successful women who could become role models. She decided to quit her teaching job, move away from her home town and work exclusively on this book. Not an easy decision. Not with four kids to raise alone.

Through these tough times, she searched out widows who would talk to her openly. What she found is extraordinary. She found not only women's pain, but more important, the depths of their sadness and poignancy of their budding hopes about the future, their sexuality, their vulnerability and at the end of it all, their power. The indomitable will these women possess is an inspiration for anyone.

This book is not intended to be strictly for widows, helping them through the worst days of loss, though it will do just that. This is a book for everyone. We know we are going to die, but we seldom come to terms with what death means and how it will affect those around us. And how many of us really know how to live? Widowhood can teach us that.

FOREWORD

These are fascinating stories, filled with raw passion and serendipitous patches of humour. Peggy Anderson and the women she writes about give a whole new perspective on death and grieving, but most of all they illuminate the art of living.

Marjorie Harris,* Toronto

---

* Author of *The Canadian Gardener* (Random House, 1990); and *Ecological Gardening* (Random House, 1991).

Preface

When my husband died in a car accident eight years ago, I became a widow. There are too many of us, wives after death, widows. Today in Canada we number close to one million. That number increases by 100,000 each year.

Contrary to public opinion, we are not all "little old ladies." Thirty seven percent of us still have half our lifetime to live after our husbands die. Contrary to public opinion, we do not "get over" our loss within the first year — or the second or the third. We feel our loss in some way for the rest of our lives. Contrary to public opinion, we do not remain forever useless appendages in a couple-oriented society, alone and unfulfilled. We move on. We change. We grow.

Luckily for the bereaved, society is learning more about death and grief. Death has become a respectable subject because special people like Elisabeth Kubler-Ross have cut away at the jungle of apathy and fear surrounding it.

Yet widowhood is still painfully difficult for most newly widowed women. Why?

First, whether death is expected or sudden it still carries with it a high voltage jolt. The minute the doctor pronounces a husband dead, the widow goes into shock. Grief moves into her life mercilessly, a physical and emotional force for which no widow is prepared. There can be no dress rehearsal for this passion play.

Secondly, despite society's new awareness about death and dying, its support for the widow is still too limited. The widow must do most of her "grief work" (the process of working through the recognized stages of grief) alone. It is the "alone" part that is the killer. She needs help!

Who can help her? Anyone who shows compassion and understanding eases the burden. But the most effective help a widow can get is from another widow. To another widow she will listen; to another widow she can talk; with another widow she may even allow herself to cry. From her she will certainly learn.

For a variety of reasons sharing amongst widows doesn't happen often or fully enough. So the widow becomes isolated in her grief. Ending this isolation through the sharing of our experiences and triumphs after a husband's death is the intent of this book. Through others' recoveries we see how grief can heal. Through others' successes we know we will have our own.

In their interviews with me, women reported that the unthinkable, the ridiculous, the debilitating, even the hilarious can happen during recovery. Yet widows cope. Meeting every kind of challenge is the collective experience of the widows I have met. They are wonderful women!

This book offers experiences for comfort and guidance. The reader can take what helps and discard the rest. One caution, however. This book does not suggest a "right" or "wrong" way for grief recovery. Rather it gives permission for all ways of grieving. Finally, this book is not just about coping with grief. It is also about the process of growth and transformation which parallels and outlives grief. To move into the process each widow, like the women in the following chapters, will need courage, determination and tenacity: the courage to be herself, the determination to seek her own solutions and the tenacity to endure the search.

Bringing women to women, facilitating their mutual sharing, healing and growth is the intent of *Wife After Death*. This project has been a labour of love for me, conceived out of my personal need and born out of the wisdom and experience of others with whom I've shared my vision.

As the following stories in this book illustrate, there are many common threads in the lives we lead after the death of a spouse.

Seeing these common threads will inspire all of us who have lost our husbands, all of us who are wives after death. But ultimately each widow will weave her own healing tapestry in her own unique fashion. That tapestry will become the fabric of her new identity.

It is my hope that *Wife After Death* will make each widow's weaving work a little lighter.

Anticipation Interrupted

Your presence touched
                    deeply
So
    deeply:
So dance-light my feet
    music-orchestrated my heart
    radiance-blushed my being
    joy-illuminated my life.

Unexpectedly
Inexplicably
Your presence ended—
Never to be experienced again.

Again
So
So
deeply touched
I now beseech Zorba:
Teach me once more to dance.

Joanne Miller, 1974

1

Peggy

anticipation interrupted

beginning comments

This chapter is my own story. I tell it first, then introduce you to other widowed women (chapters two to seven) who have been significant role models in my own healing and growth.

"PEGGY" tells where I was before and immediately after the death of my husband.

PEGGY

I am alone. I see my husband stretched on a cold steel bed shrouded to the shoulders in white hospital sheets. 'Wrapped in swaddling bands' sings through my brain. But this is not a new beginning. This is an end.

I move closer. He looks as if he is asleep. But his neck is puffed out abnormally. And though he is still warm, he is absolutely still.

I do not sit. I do not hold him. I stand by his body, frightened. It is all so unreal. I am not prepared to encounter death so soon.

Bob is now a shell, a corpse, no longer vibrant. I had loved his body! It had planted four incredibly beautiful children in me and had given me more loving than I might ever have again. Yet I leave it here, too soon, discarding it like an old piece of garbage.

God, I wish I had stayed with him longer; looked at him; held him; felt his spirit leaving. This was an intimacy, our last time together, of another dimension. And it was much more uncomfortable than our first sexual experience.

I had loved him. He was gone.

My husband was my first man. When I was in grade ten and he was in grade thirteen we dated a little. He was a nice guy, good-looking and sensitive. It was obvious that he loved

3

me even then. He reported how he agonized about calling me, fearing rejection. We were both only in high school. I wasn't impressed and wanted to play the field. Certainly it was not love at first sight for me.

But Bob continued to see me when he returned home from university on the occasional weekend. Our friendship grew.

I decided after grade thirteen to go to University of Toronto where Bob was by now in first year law. We saw a lot of each other. By the end of my first year we had become intimate and loved each other passionately. We decided by the middle of October in my second year to get married that Christmas.

There was stress involved in being students and newlyweds — I liked to study, he liked to make love. But we worked it through. After graduation instead of teaching I got pregnant, joyfully. Bob wanted a family. He thought that if he waited much longer he would be too old. He was twenty-six! We moved to Stratford, began our family and Bob started his law career.

Gradually, as our family grew, our lives became child centred. Occasionally we made time just for ourselves. Weekends away or trips south rekindled the fires of passion between us.

After about ten years of mothering our three children I felt I needed to be out in the work force, to be myself, separate from the children; Bob encouraged me to return to teaching. He would help with the children, with groceries and a house-keeper so that I could make use of my skills and feel that I, too, had a contribution to make to society. I taught high school English for a year and a half and was on the verge of getting a permanent certificate when I became pregnant with our fourth and last child, Sarah.

I was very happy about this situation. It had been a long time since I'd had a baby to hold in my arms. I loved that part of mothering. When the three older children were six, eight and ten, Sarah was born.

I left teaching to stay at home with Sarah but three years later, when Sarah needed me less, I took evening courses in Special Education and when a local elementary school offered me a position, I started teaching again. Bob was understanding and supportive of my decision, even though my working meant we had less time together as a family.

Our lives then were busy, bordering on the frenzied. Because I was working and finding the switch from secondary to elementary teaching difficult, Bob spent more time with us than usual.

All five of us benefitted from his care and attention. Our children had a Dad who truly loved them and preferred to be with them over anything else.

I remember how extremely proud Bob was of all his children; how proud he was that his first born child was a son; how pleased he was about Jeff's ability to stand up for himself in schoolyard fights. He was overjoyed when Matt made the all-star hockey team two years in a row. Bob and Matt became inseparable, going to practices and to out of town games.

In Bob's eyes, the girls were special. He loved Cathy dearly. He respected her intelligence, her athletic ability and her individuality. He feared her stubborn streak and felt better able to deal with all of Jeff's antics than with a Cathy 'digging in her heels.' When Cathy won the coveted Hamlet school 'H' as best student in public school, I called him at the office to tell him and he cried over the phone, he was so happy.

Of course, Sarah, our baby and our last child, was his favourite. He loved to play with her, to take her out for walks or tobogganing or skiing at three; on business trips with him at five.

All four children lost a lot when their father died.

In the few years before Bob's death, we were beginning to feel many strains in our lives. The economy of Stratford was depressed. There were problems in the law firm in which Bob was a partner and Bob felt it horribly. He developed a skin rash and itchy eyes. I think he hated going to the office.

Then, Bob's Dad died. The old law firm reorganized and Bob began his own practice. By the time of the car accident, two years later, he was feeling physically and emotionally good — independent and proud — even though we were broke.

So that's where I was just before Bob's death. A mom, a wife, a teacher; busy, worried, but okay. We were pulling together as a family. Better things were on the way. Or so I believed at the time.

Our last weekend together was special. On Grey Cup weekend we farmed out the kids and retreated to Niagara-on-the-Lake for time alone. It was wonderful. We relaxed around the fireplace in our room, lingered over dinner and made love.

During the Saturday afternoon we had walked up and down the main street sometimes together, sometimes apart, shopping for early Christmas presents.

As Bob walked toward me just outside a bakery, he caught my eye and on coming closer said a strange thing which in retrospect has been wonderful.

'I want you to know that being with you has made my life worthwhile.'

Interesting that he chose to tell me this then, in the last week of his life.

The weather December 6, the day of the accident, was beautiful. No snow on the roads, sun in the sky. Early that morning Bob brought me a cup of tea as I dressed for school. He was going to Kitchener to search a title. I planned to do my own parent interviews at my school then at 3:30 visit our children's teachers. Bob was to meet me if he could. I was not surprised when he didn't show; I assumed he was busy at work. I got home at 4:30.

At 5:30 the phone rang. Bob had been in a car accident. A car had been out passing in Bob's lane and had hit him head on. The nurse emphasized he was fine, had a broken leg, no head injuries. Nothing serious.

Satisfied that it was not an emergency, I did not rush. When I arrived at the hospital I was too late, although I didn't know that as I walked calmly through the automatically opened doors to the emergency ward at 6:45.

A policeman stopped me to talk to me. It seemed that the boys in the other car had been treated and released. When I asked, 'But Bob's going to be all right, isn't he?' the policeman said, 'He has a fifty-fifty chance.' That was the first moment I had any idea that Bob was even seriously injured!

Things deteriorated from then on. A nurse came out and said that I couldn't see my husband just yet. She then ushered me into a room. *The Quiet Room* read the sign over the door. The sign was ominous. I was scared. I knew Bob's life was in danger.

Then the nurse returned to tell us Bob had gone into cardiac arrest and that the doctors were doing everything they could for him. I still didn't expect death. We were in a modern hospital, after all.

I felt that I had to be alone and asked directions to the washroom where I sat and prayed. I wanted my husband to live. I was not a praying person but I was willing to make a deal with God now.

It didn't work. The doctor met me back in *The Quiet Room*. He was cold and callous. He told me that Bob was dead, that Bob had been in great pain and that they had not expected he would die. The doctor did not say 'We did everything we could for him.' And they didn't, as far as I could tell when the facts were all gathered later at an inquest.

At the time, though, I felt no anger, nothing; just disbelief, shock.

When I finally did get into the emergency room I felt like my mind was totally disassociated from my body. I was numb; I left as quickly as I could.

After Bob's death I was in a kind of fog. Some incidents are crystal clear in my mind while others are blank. It's strange to look at what my memory has selected. What, I wonder, did it discard, repress?

I clearly recall making all the funeral arrangements myself. I knew exactly what I needed. Privacy. We had always valued privacy in our family and I hated it, that the accident was front page news and everyone knew, or thought they knew, what had happened. I didn't even know! We had a ritual visitation, with a closed casket, private funeral and interment. That was perfect for us.

During the visitation my older three children Jeff, Cathy and Matthew were with me. I cried once or twice but basically I was 'a brick.' Flowers, cards and donations poured in. It was overwhelming. I came to hate the sight of flowers.

I remember with such clarity when the kids and I were viewing the open casket, Jeff's tucking a dollar bill under Bob's hand because he owed his Dad money and wanted to clear his debts with him. I remember, too, Matt's putting his hockey 'hat trick' pin — a little Snoopy with a hockey stick — in the coffin on his Dad's chest. These things Matt and Jeff did spontaneously, their last communication with their Father.

Another memory comes from the morning of the funeral. I couldn't remember where I had left my dress boots. I went to the funeral and cemetery after it, wearing battered old mukluks and elegant fur coat! I didn't care. That was the first time in my life that I knew what you wore didn't matter. At that time nothing mattered, but the fact that Bob was dead.

Physically, during the funeral I was healthy, almost glowing, but totally in shock. After the funeral I was a mess. Outwardly I looked thin and tired. I could not sleep, had no desire to eat, felt exhausted, jumpy, and couldn't walk a block or shop an hour — quite unlike myself. I was totally drained. I developed heart pains and thought I would have a heart attack.

I did some unusual things. For instance, every day in the first few weeks while my sister was staying with me I would collect the sympathy cards from the mail box, take them upstairs to my bedroom, run a bath, get in, open the mail and cry with the bath running so Liz could not hear me sob. I kept my grief to myself.

I also bought an electric blanket; I hated the cold empty bed. I had to have warmth with me or I couldn't sleep. I remember thinking one night, soon after Bob died, when I switched the blanket control to 'off' how like life that blanket was. When death switches the current of life off, the body, like my comfortless blue blanket, goes cold, without spirit or vitality;

unloving, unconscious matter; a thing to be returned to the earth.

I remember that Bob's death altered many of my usual perceptions. For example, immediately after his death, time seemed to stand still; each minute seemed like an hour in my life. Instead of having too little time on my hands as I always had in the past, I now had too much. I couldn't sit still doing nothing. I had to have the radio on, even when I went to sleep at night. Silence brought fear. Being alone without noise was unbearable.

I also lost my ability to concentrate or remember. I would turn on the stove element to make tea then forget what I had done. I would take a pill and minutes later not remember taking it. I had to write down absolutely everything or I would forget. I had so much business to do at this time it's a wonder I made any logical decisions at all.

Yet in other ways I became very clear, almost omniscient. I knew, for instance, unquestionably, what was important in life after Bob's death. It was as if scales fell from my eyes and I saw clearly for the first time. I knew that health and loving and children were precious; that money and power and position were nothing.

So the children became the focus of my life. Bob and I had loved them. Now I would raise them alone. My maxim became 'Do what's best for the kids.' This made some decision making very simple for me. When it became obvious in January that I didn't have the energy to teach and parent, I knew that I had to take a leave from my job. Before this I would have put my work first. Now I knew better.

Soon after Bob's death I knew, too, that I was vulnerable and could easily become dependent. In the lawyer's office about three weeks after the funeral with my Dad on one side of me and my brother-in-law on the other, I said,

> I want you to know that I need your advice but I also want
> you to know that I have to make the decisions myself. If I screw
> up, I screw up. But I am going to be in charge of the rest of
> my life.

As weak as I was then, I knew that this realization was basic to my future survival.

Decisions were now up to me. I had never paid bills, budgeted, made loans, worked out taxes. With insurance money coming in and a business to terminate, I had to become investment conscious and tax law wise. My mind seemed to be mush. Could I cope?

Well, the truth of the matter is there was no one else to do it. So I did.

I was learning through my shock. My numbed brain was striving to assimilate new information and to adjust to new kinds of thinking processes. My mind cushioned some blows but it often made good sense out of the overload of information coming into it. It stood up well for me in this crucial time.

My mind, however, could be my enemy. Anxieties which seemed to hinder my recovery surfaced immediately after Bob's death. I was very protective of the children. Overprotective. It was a Stratford winter. Bad storms. Matt was on a travelling hockey team; Jeff had friends who drove. Sarah and Cathy sometimes needed chauffeuring. I was petrified that one of the children would die in a car accident.

When Matt was about to leave with friends for an out of town hockey game a few days after Bob died, it was excruciatingly difficult for me to let him go out into the storm in a vehicle which could kill. I was so certain that I would never see him again. But I knew that he must never know this; I had to let him go.

I was terrified of getting into a car, even as a passenger. Every car I saw coming toward me I viewed as a potential killer. I could not drive for a while. Then I would drive a little, but just in town. When I had to travel to the cottage fifty miles away to get it ready to sell a month after Bob's car accident, I was certain that I couldn't last one hour in highway traffic. So I took a friend with me. She would drive when I flaked. But I DID drive one way. And that was a significant victory for me.

When I continued to fear that a vehicle would come out of

the passing lane and hit me I discussed this with a psychiatrist. He assured me that my fear was perfectly normal. As he put it, 'In the forest if a tree falls on someone you love and it kills them, you naturally think that another tree will fall.' It helped to know this. My anxieties about driving disappeared soon after that.

I was also anxious about death. I feared my own death, experienced heart pains and worried about the kids being orphaned, until my physician assured me my heart was strong and my fears normal.

Death, which I had never even noticed before, bothered me elsewhere: on T.V. (the police shoot-outs, the mad car chases out of which everyone escapes alive, and the hospital shows), on stage and in opera. They toyed with death. I couldn't even watch the televised version of Stratford's 'The Mikado', although just a few months before, Bob and I had loved the stage version. Death was so near and awful for me that even its artificial reproduction was too difficult for me to witness.

Somehow, I had to come to terms with this death; I had to learn about it firsthand. This was no small curiosity I held. It was an overwhelming compulsion within me which I could not ignore or reject.

So I began to feed my compulsion with reading. I read books to confirm that my emotions were normal; books to promise better times. Books to give me faith and hope. Books by psychologists, philosophers, doctors and scientists. Books by courageous people who had terminal illnesses. I read, voraciously, everything I could find.

Immediately after Bob's death, when I had no ability to concentrate, a skinny book called *Good Grief* said the right things for that time and said them clearly and concisely. As time passed, my ability to stay with a book grew and I needed more answers. I moved into self-help type literature then eventually into more complex material.

I read *Beginnings* by Wylie and *Widow* and *Lifelines* by Caine and Kushner's inspirational book, *When Bad Things Happen to Good People*; Earl Grollman's, *Talking About Death* and

What Helped Me When My Loved One Died and Hinton's *Dying*. All of the books by Elisabeth Kubler-Ross, this century's leading authority on death, dying and bereavement I found riveting. Moody's book, *Life After Life*, about near death experiences, C. S. Lewis' *A Grief Observed* and his *Problem of Pain* all added to my knowledge and understanding.

To acquaint myself with the children's grief process I read *Learning to Say Good-by* by Eda LeShan and by Jill Krementz, *How It Feels When a Parent Dies*.

I needed desperately to read in order to come to terms with my loss. I needed to know why. Not so much why my husband died. But 'Why life?' To put meaning back into my life at a time when I was a broken shell, hating people and life and God, I had to read.

During all this it helped me to know that I was loved. Mom and Dad, my sister and her husband were available for moral support at any time night or day. They could not stay with me in my home but they were near as a telephone call. The phone calls kept me sane. Eventually, I began to regain my strength and my mental equilibrium.

Part of my finding that balance came from exploring and accepting my new identity. That process would not occur quickly. At first I didn't really understand what 'Bob is dead' meant, let alone what being a widow would entail. At the funeral I saw the body, shook the hands, observed the flowers, buried the coffin. But nothing was real. It was all like a very slow motion picture in which I knew the characters but could not feel the pain. I was removed, cushioned with shock really, and so when all the ritual ended and the relatives went, I was left with dead flowers and a very tenuous understanding of the situation.

I knew with my head that Bob was dead but I hadn't really felt his loss. For a very long time I lived as though he were still alive but absent, away on an extended business trip. I kept the 'wife' alive. I knew that I had to string up the clothes line and take out the garbage myself, but subconsciously, I rejected the fact that Bob was really gone. Someday he would return and get me out of this awful mess. I continued to feel his presence, thinking as I made decisions for our family, 'Bob would approve of this, make this choice, buy that.'

So he lived in my life for some time after his death because I wanted it that way. I kept him alive for myself in many little ways: the electric blanket at bedtime and the radio's chatter for company. With strangers I would talk as if I were still a wife with a husband. A woman alone in the world was not safe, I thought, and I'd be damned if I would let anyone know I was without a man. I didn't tell people I was a 'widow.' I hated the sound of the word, let alone the meaning.

Of course, I couldn't go on being the wife of a man who did not exist. Eventually, I began to do things which gradually broke the 'wife' pattern and freed me to get on with being the widow I was.

Bob's suits and shirts hung in his closet and sat in his drawers for months and months after his death. Then one day the 'widow' took over and cleared everything out. She became very assertive in other areas too, chipping away at the wife until, bit by bit, the wife disappeared. It was the widow who began sleeping in the whole bed and who eventually chucked the queen sized bed out entirely. Who needed it? Not the widow. It was the widow who took off the wedding ring, though the wife feared family disapproval. The widow knew better. It was the widow who began to circulate again with other adults and planned an adventure in backpacking through Europe with the children. The widow was getting feisty. Through all this it was as if the wife were observing, anticipating that the widow would stumble and fall. But my widow was strong and with each success she grew a little stronger still.

There were setbacks. I continued to hide the fact that I was a widow in situations where people did not know me. For a long time I couldn't speak the truth and may not ever have done it had I not made a career change and moved to a bigger city.

When I left the town in which Bob and I had raised the children, I left the wife there too. Almost four years after Bob died, now in London, I began to write this book and the first words I put on paper were:

> I am a widow. I have been a widow for almost four years. It is rare for me to state it; impossible to write it.

That was literally true. It had taken me four years to admit to myself that I was a widow living alone. Now, in the seventh year of my widowhood, I am just becoming aware of all the ramifications of that aloneness. But I can say, 'Peggy Anderson is by herself with her children in the world because her husband died.' I have finally made the leap 'from wife to widow.'

Although I had come to terms with my aloneness, it was 'alone without a man' I meant when I said 'alone.' In truth, I had not been 'alone' at all after Bob's death. I had always had my four children to keep me company. They were a blessing, but in time they would push me past my limits and force me into new growth.

It was not an easy first four years for us. Bob died Monday, December 6th. Three days later, on the day of the funeral, Jeff turned fifteen. Cathy turned thirteen three days after that. Matt and Sarah were eleven and five respectively. My life would be child centred and child driven for some time.

Initially each of the children reacted differently to losing a father. The day after Bob's death Sarah went off to nursery school. The others stayed at home. Cathy, always the organizer, decided to keep a record of wonderful neighbours and friends who brought us food. I looked at the list a few days later and had to laugh at an unexpected entry. It read:

Briggs   chicken   (dead)

Cathy had kept her sense of humour, even at this awful time!

But the same morning Jeff was not so controlled. Before I left for the funeral home he was hysterical, believing he had caused his Dad's death. In his mind because he had helped pick out the car Bob drove in the accident, Jeff felt responsible. My brother offered to take Jeff to the crash site. Jeff saw the ditch where fire fighters had struggled with the jaws of life to get Bob out of the wreck. He also saw that there was an incline in the road. His Dad coming to that hump would not have been able to see the oncoming car until almost too late. Jeff needed that trip. He had to know first hand how and where the accident happened. This trip helped alleviate his earlier hysteria.

In contrast to his older brother, Matt was quiet. And sensitive. No one asked him to go to the scene of the accident and he was hurt (I only learned much later) because he felt left out. He was also very concerned about me and tried to cheer me up by telling me a joke one night before bed. I listened while he told about a pig with a peg leg, the very last joke Bob had recounted to the family. And Matt told it word for word, inflection for inflection as his Dad had only nights before. Like a physical shock it hit me that Matt would never learn another joke, another anything from his Dad.

Sarah was a grown up five when Bob died. I don't know how much death was real to her then. During the funeral she asked questions but was very well behaved. When things bothered her after that, she would simply cry. She, too, was hurting. A trip to Loblaw's beside the funeral home made her cry. A song on the radio, *The Wreck of the Edmund Fitzgerald* brought unexpected tears because it was 'Daddy's favourite song,' she said. At least Sarah cried!

Our oldest daughter, Cathy, was just the opposite. She never broke stride, never let go. She seemed brittle. I couldn't touch her, hug her. She hated to see me cry and told me so, adding that she thought I was 'crazy.' At the outset, denial was her way of dealing with her grief.

As time passed, family dynamics changed. My son, Jeff,

became a great help at home, shopping and cooking when I was too tired after work to move. But eventually he began to test the new situation. Now fifteen he started to behave irresponsibly, I thought, wanting more privileges and ever later weekend curfews. We clashed violently over this. He became verbally abusive. I would lose my temper or cry. Things got worse. Jeff's belligerence began to affect the younger children. I watched as Matt and Cathy became mouthy, constantly questioning my authority. In time I had no self-esteem left.

Near Christmas two years after Bob's death I told Jeff he must live by my rules or leave. I think he expected me to change my mind. I did not, although that was one of the hardest decisions of my lifetime. After he left, I felt like a failure, cried for nights on end. But gradually I saw that the rest of our family was benefitting from Jeff's absence. We were peaceful. We could do things together without tension. There was only one adult in the house and she was in control. Because Jeff had been offered a place to stay with my parents I knew he was safe. My parents had rules which Jeff didn't question. His manners improved. He studied at night. His marks went up. He took a job, did well at it and got lots of positive strokes from his boss. In time I could see that our separation gave us both a chance to grow and heal in our own ways.

Now it was Matt's turn. Quiet Matthew who bottled up all his feelings until I thought it would kill him. Matt and his Dad had a special relationship. After Bob's death I tried to be hockey Mom and Dad both for Matt, went to all his all-star games and tournaments. It was wonderful to be with the team parents. They were good friends through a bad time.

But the following September, Matt was cut from the team. He lost his hockey 'family' on top of losing his Dad. By Christmas he had developed severe and long lasting migraines. He began biting his knuckles until they became swollen and blue. He became secretive and withdrawn. School suffered. He didn't communicate with me much and when he did he was always angry.

It became frighteningly apparent when Matt ended up in

hospital that he was forming self-destructive patterns. I was worried sick and paranoid about his actions and friends as a result. I asked for help from a friend of my husband's who worked with adolescents. He emphasized that despite my fear, I would have to show Matthew that I loved and trusted him. He also was adamant that I should not send Matt away to school, an option which in my panic I had considered. Matt needed to be with me and to know that I loved him and trusted him. And so I tried loving Matt through his anger.

There were many tense times between us, but we gradually began to talk. We discussed how it felt for him to lose a Dad. He admitted his anger against me, believing his grief was greater than mine because 'to lose a Dad is worse than to lose a husband.' He admitted that a recurring dream in which he saw his Dad on the couch but couldn't get him to talk, haunted him. He felt abandoned when no one saw his pain; when no one reached out to help. So he 'put on a front.'

It shocks me now to realize that because of my own sadness I was unable to recognize the manifestations of grief in Matt and the others.

The children are now years older and wiser, and so am I. We are all living together in London. Jeff is attending first year Law School at Western. Cathy is finishing a Political Science degree at U.W.O. and has been accepted into Law at U.B.C. Matt, on leave from studying before university next year, has just left for five months of camping and backpacking in Australia. Sarah is in grade eight. They are well adjusted, happy, healthy kids. And we are a caring, communicating, normal family.

I believe we have reached a level of tolerance and love among ourselves which could not have existed without our experiencing and overcoming loss and grief. In a very real way, Bob's death has become, for each one of us, a gift of life.

There would be challenges other than children to test me and to encourage my growth as woman during my healing process. One of these was in the area of my sexuality. My husband was my first and until just recently my only man. I had never made love to any man before my husband and probably wouldn't have been with another man in my life had Bob not died. I expected to be monogamous in our marriage and so did he and we were.

In the sexuality department as in the rest of my life before Bob's death I allowed things to happen to me. I did not shape them for myself. I did not choose to take responsibility for my body or my life, then blamed my husband when things did not work out well in either category.

Discovering my own sexuality parallelled my discovering myself and both discoveries came as a direct result of my husband's death. Early in my widowhood I had no contact with men except through business or work and these men were either married, octogenarians or relatives! For a year or two after Bob died that was all right because I was not at all interested in being with another man. I believed I would never love again; remarriage was unthinkable. I would remain forever loyal to my husband. Celibacy was what I needed and wanted — at first.

In the early stage of my widowhood I was frantically busy nurturing the children, doing my job and organizing the household. I also kept a tight rein on my emotions. I was flat — like a taut string ready to break at any moment but somehow unable to loosen the tension which my situation produced. It was necessary for me to change or break.

First, because I loved music and dancing I began an aerobics class and found I enjoyed keeping in shape. Exercising made me feel better and for the first time I became aware of my body in a new way. I also began to do things outside for my own pleasure. I took up cross country skiing and gardening and sunning. Being outside and active paid dividends. It eased the stress and lightened my emotional load considerably. Another option I turned to for my own pleasure was music. I had always loved playing the piano and again in an effort to nurture myself

I began taking music lessons. Practising allowed me to tune out everything, almost like a meditation. I could also let some of my repressed passion express itself in the music. So when I couldn't sleep at night, and that was often, I would either get up and exercise to music or play the piano for an hour or so. Not the same kind of release as love making but a positive substitute for that void! My new activities also led the way to my quiet inner centre. For me, physical exercise, nature and music alleviated stress and stimulated personal growth.

As time passed I began to feel less that I had to remain faithful to my husband. He was dead; I was still alive. Now I wanted a good relationship with another man once more. Along with this discovery, however, was the disturbing fact that I was becoming more and more ill at ease with the opposite sex. I was terrified that a man might walk into my life. The recognition that what I yearned for deeply was also my greatest fear scared me. I knew that I had a problem.

As life often does, it presented me with a scenario in which I could work out that problem. My first date. I was surprised and pleased when a man whom I knew casually and who was not yet married (as most men my age were) asked me out. My imagination blew the whole event way out of proportion. This man was perfect for me, I thought, a knight in shining armour. That fantasy, plus the fact that I had not been alone with an available man for three years and my last date was about twenty-five years ago, unnerved me. But I wasn't going to miss this opportunity!

Our date was for dinner at his house. I took the soup. Good thing I made it beforehand. I was very nervous! One vodka and orange juice into the evening and I was gone. It was all I could do to carry on a conversation and get through the meal. The man was a perfect gentleman although obviously I was both afraid and excited by the prospect that maybe he wouldn't be. When that first date turned out to be our last I was distraught. I convinced myself that because he didn't call back I was unlovable, that I had 'blown it' and that I would remain partnerless forever.

I was overreacting and fortunately friends who knew what had happened gently encouraged me to remain open to future opportunities. And so eventually I was ready to try again. Then another block. There were no men available, at least where I hung out, which was mostly in my own kitchen! There I stayed in my comfortable shell, closed up, expecting to die partnerless.

In the winter of my third widowed year I decided I needed some adult company. I was 'children' and 'alone' burned out. I decided to attend a retreat weekend which had been recommended to me. I would be away from friends and family for the first time since Bob's death. It was a big risk. I didn't like to do things alone and never had. For this weekend I would have to drive to a remote schoolhouse alone, be with adults whom I had never met before, socialize and later share deep emotions with strangers. The first of these things I hadn't done since Bob's death three years ago; the last I had probably never done in my lifetime.

Could I do it? Fortunately the leaders of the retreat knew their business. They made a task which seemed almost insurmountable to me easier by creating a loving community atmosphere.

During that weekend we shared personal stories, meditation, writing and celebration in an effort to explore ourselves. That was the easy part. The most difficult part which no one had explained to me beforehand (if they had, I wouldn't have been there), was the individual experiential component of the weekend. In an intense one-on-one session with a leader each person was expected to confront his or her most pressing problem. My issues were repressed anger and debilitating guilt, both related to the death of my husband. In essence my work was 'grief work.'

When I realized what was happening here I became so frightened I couldn't eat and didn't sleep. I knew I could have opted out. Yet I had come to this retreat desperately searching for something. Either stubborn will or innate courage compelled me to 'go for it.' My work involved reliving the most painful experience I had from the period around Bob's death. The worst time had been that hour in the hospital during and after Bob's cardiac arrest and my not getting to see him. When I 'returned' to that time and place in my mind, I hated. I hated the nurses for not telling me how ill Bob was and the policeman for stalling me at the emergency door so that I could not get to be with my husband before he died. I hated the doctor for telling me Bob was dead, and Bob's mother for demanding his rings minutes after his death. Most of all, I hated myself. I hated myself because I had not been there for my husband when he needed me most, when he was in pain and dying.

Reliving that hospital experience, changing it so that I could be with Bob before he died, saying what I would like to have said to him, was my work. The process was like the snake's shedding old restrictive skin, painful but renewing. I cried, I laughed, but I felt it totally. Best of all, I was not alone. I had support from everyone present.

There was magic in that weekend retreat for all of us who shared our brokenness and our healing. For me there was another magic. During that weekend I 'fell in love.' That love was reciprocated only on a platonic level. He was married and we were sensible. Yet through it I learned a lesson important for my future. I learned that I could love and be loved once more and, someday, I knew I would have a man in my life again.

I went home from the retreat ready to take stock. I was a forty year old woman raising four children alone. I was managing. But I knew clearly that I could not handle another child. I also knew that I wanted to share my life again with a man. Saying 'no' to more children but 'yes' to a man meant that I had to begin to think about birth control — now. Not in the heat of a passionate moment but now, when I felt very clearly my own needs.

So for the first time after Bob's death and with no mate even close on the horizon, I decided to take charge of my own sexuality. I visited a doctor and ordered a diaphragm. When I found that uncomfortable and awkward I began to consider a tubal ligation. Fearing hospitals more than was normal because of the circumstances of Bob's death, I wondered why I would risk putting my life on the line in order to reap some nebulous sexual pleasure in the future. Funny though. I had to do it. I had to take my needs and responsibilities as a woman seriously.

Having the operation was a milestone for me. I overcame a very real fear of death. And I admitted to myself that my sexuality was important. It was the first in a series of events in my life which would gradually see me change.

After that my life became busier. I made some important career changes and planned to leave our home town. The children and I moved away from familiarity and family to begin again, alone. We had to rely on our own resources for awhile in this strange town and consequently we began to be more supportive of each other. I felt good about my decision; after a few acclimatization problems the kids began to thrive. My positive attitude grew. Now I was finally directing my own life and proud of it! New work and new friends in my new community made my living both interesting and challenging. Through mutual friends I met and dated a few men occasionally. That was good. I had no expectations and was much less tense about future and outcome. If I met a man who wasn't interesting I could refuse a second date. If a man dated me once and didn't call back, I understood. That was not rejection but mutual incompatibility. I also developed a few good platonic men friends with whom I would talk on the phone or join for lunch. I was more relaxed now in the company of men and was beginning to feel more balanced about the need for partnering again. I was beginning to really love life once more!

2

Betty

footprints in the snow

beginning comments

When I became a widow suddenly after Bob's death, I had no idea what widowhood meant. I was totally unprepared to be a widow. In my life I had known only two widows, both much older than I. The first was my Great Aunt Betty whose husband died when he was in his late seventies. My Aunt was always strong; she had her faith. When she was widowed she seemed to cope well. I was thirty when her husband died, busy being a new mother and fond wife. I had no idea how it would be to lose a husband after forty years together. What did she feel? I did not ask. Bob and I went to the funeral, then visited her occasionally up north during our summer vacations. I could have done more.

When Bob died eight years later, Aunt Betty came and stayed with me, helping with the unpacking of countless cartons of books from our enforced move three months after Bob's death. I was still in shock. Her presence kept me going.

Now my aunt is a busy woman. Her daily schedule begins by exercising half an hour with Ed Allen and can include anything after that from picking up mail for handicapped friends to participating in a prayer group, working at the Hospital Auxiliary, playing bridge or bowling. Her day ends around midnight, after T.V. and quilting, with writing, reading and quiet prayer. A normal active life for a young woman these days. The unusual thing about this schedule is that the woman who keeps it turned eighty-eight this September!

Betty does not look her age and she certainly does not act 'old.' She has always liked to keep busy! She has sent dozens of her handmade quilts (two at a time) to the Scott Mission over the last ten years. Every morning she reads the Toronto Star cover to cover. She networks with single older women keeping in touch daily for mutual company and safety. Betty is physically, mentally and emotionally on top of things.

She is a strong woman with a strong faith whose personal analysis of life is that it is pretty wonderful, even when you are alone. Here is her story.

BETTY

I was born in 1902. Religion played an important role in my family as I grew up. Dad had three brothers, Uncle Wesley, Uncle Cebe and Uncle Henry who were all ministers of the Evangelical Church. My Dad was not a minister but he was a church leader; he'd take prayer meetings Wednesday nights in the Evangelical Church and regularly at home. I remember his telling us that at one of his Wednesday meetings he was sitting beside a man who felt he couldn't give his life to Christ because he had a pipe in his pocket! As long as he had that pipe in his pocket he didn't feel free. My Dad let him give his life to Christ anyway, pipe or no pipe.

While I was growing up, nightly prayer meetings were routine. I and my mother and four brothers and sisters would sit in the room while Dad would read from the bible and say a prayer. I can't go into details about the event — that was sixty or seventy years ago, but I do know that his prayers included everything that happened to be on his mind at the time plus, of course, his concerns for his family. On Sundays we went to church in the morning and Sunday school in the afternoon and church at night. Sunday was a special day in our family because we didn't do anything on Sundays that we'd do every day. We could read or go for a walk. I spent a lot of time with my friends those Sundays. We didn't play cards or dance in my family. Cards were gambling. Dancing was worse. Anybody I knew just didn't dance. My parents didn't dance.

Rules in the family came more from my Dad than from the church. He could be strict. As a child I knew inside that I was trying to live according to the rules of the bible and the rules of my father. I did things because I knew they were right to do and because I wanted to live up to the expectations of others. For instance, way back seventy or eighty years ago when I would have been ten or younger, I was shocked to find that my brother had been dancing. I thought that was awful. I guess my disapproval came from my family and the church. When I grew up I felt differently about it. I remember going to a dance with a chap from Waterloo College who was going through for the Lutheran ministry. This was my first and only dance and I was like a stick. You have to learn to dance and I hadn't. I don't have dancing feet. I didn't do it again. But as you can see my ideas about dancing did change.

In terms of my relationship with God, though, apart from the rules of the bible, I have always had a feeling inside that I'm not alone. I never will fully understand that feeling although my understanding has grown over the years. This is not a feeling that everyone shares. My husband was not religious and did not have that kind of faith. His family was not church going. He went to a young men's Sunday school class and eventually taught a class of boys after we were married. He went along with me to church for a long time until his health got in the way. I think he believed in God and in the church. But he didn't have that inside feeling that I felt. And I tried not to judge.

I married Roy in 1927. We were married forty-seven years and had a daughter, Barbara, who is now an anesthesiologist. When Roy was twenty-seven and I was twenty-eight we began a retail clothing business. We were very young when you think of it now and neither Roy nor his partner had very much money but the business succeeded. We expanded from a little store to a big one, then into a resort town in the summer and up north into Gravenhurst, Bigwin Inn and Bracebridge over the years. Finally, when Roy's health became an issue we settled in Bracebridge where the climate was better for his breathing.

In our earlier years together we sort of went our own ways. We had different interests. There were a few things I did just for Roy. One was riding. Roy had his own horse for years. I rode a slow nag which was fine for me but I was scared all the time I was on him. I never did enjoy riding. I'd go with Roy golfing too, but I didn't golf very much myself. I tried it only once. If he didn't have men to go with him I'd go. We always went in a cart and I'd drive the cart and watch. Also, Roy loved to plan trips and we had a number of those. It was really his pleasure and I enjoyed Europe but I wouldn't go now on a bet.

I have always been involved in church work, teaching Sunday school and doing bazaar work. As I've said, family Sundays were church oriented. It has always been my feeling that Sundays should be special. If I didn't get some cleaning done during the week I certainly wasn't going to do it on a Sunday. Recently I have been on the church board and involved in a prayer group affiliated with our church. I don't know how I could live without my church and my faith.

In my life I have always felt a spiritual link with God which gives me peace. One night this winter that link was put to a test. I wakened at four o'clock in the morning and I thought I heard my doorbell. It rang just once so I thought maybe it was a dream. But it bothered me. I didn't know whether to get up and look. I would never open the door. I didn't want to look either. So I just said an extra prayer and rolled over and went back to sleep, just like that. It was amazing because ordinarily I think I would have stayed awake and wondered. The next morning, since I was curious about whether it was a dream or not, I checked outside. There were footprints in the snow right up to my door. It's beyond my power to feel so unworried about such a thing. So that was an example of my faith.

Roy's illness was a test of my faith in a way too. When he was in his late sixties he became ill. His chronic asthma turned into emphysema. The last few years we tried going south to help him with his breathing but eventually the disease took its toll. I cared for him in his illness. I didn't think of nursing him as a burden. After all the years we lived together there are things that you just do. It's natural. I can remember the stress he was under — I can still see him sitting there in his big chair just gasping for breath — and saying, 'God, why can't I die?' An earlier death would have been a relief for him. Better than lingering on and on with nothing ahead of him. So when he did die I was not unhappy for him. It was for the best.

In a way my husband helped me prepare for being alone while he was ill. He didn't ever feel that I should stay home with him because he was not feeling very well. He thought

I should get out. If he had resented my going I would have stopped all these things and then where would I have been? His supportiveness prepared me to be alone.

Nevertheless, after his death the realization that I was all alone was with me all the time. I missed having him here to discuss things with me. I missed male companionship. If there is a way to fill the gap of missing that male conversation that goes when a husband dies I haven't managed to find it. Couples rarely invite a single person out to dinner.

After Roy's death I kept the same friends, interests and activities but the centre of my energies went to doing something for others now rather than for my husband. As I am getting older I feel very fortunate to have my health. I have arthritis in my little finger but otherwise I am very healthy. Having my health means so much to me because it allows me to get out and help others less fortunate and that is what has always given my life meaning. One of my friends gets very low and she wonders how long she will be living. Well, all that passes through my mind sometimes as well, but I don't dwell on it. I just take a day at a time.

Part of my being able to accept Roy's death and go on comes, I think, from having a strong faith. I'd feel lost without the church. I attend church services on Sundays and a bible study group on Thursday mornings: these things renew my faith. In the Thursday group there are eighteen of us. I'm the only one my age in it but I feel right at home and very close to everyone there. Although we follow a course outline and have books and homework related to various religious topics, we don't always stick to the curriculum. If any member has anything he or she feels a need to have discussed or a prayer said in the group, the leader puts that person in the centre of the circle. We put hands on the head of the person in need and offer our prayers spoken or silent. I'm not one to talk out loud. I can pray silently, in my heart. But we help each other in this way. We can totally trust each other there in that group. Going to church, the prayer group and people renew my faith.

There are a lot of things that I can't do but I like doing the things I am doing for people who need help. Making quilts for the Scott Mission. That gives me a satisfaction. I think I'm not just wasting my time at night watching T.V. I can still help someone who is in need. At night I always go to sleep thinking, 'What worthwhile project can I do tomorrow?' If there are other people who are less fortunate than I am and if taking them out or going to visit them is something they enjoy, then I get a nice feeling about it, too. I think that is valuable. Not in terms of money; valuable because it gives me a nice feeling.

Occasionally, I wonder what is going to happen to me when I get old. I hope I pass on just like that, rather than having to go into a home or a hospital somewhere. But you do not always have the choice. I just live one day at a time.

concluding comments

Betty came from a very strongly religious background. Church and faith coloured her upbringing, filled her life and facilitated her grief work after the death of her husband. Like many widows, Betty clearly missed her husband. But she accepted death for him as part of God's plan, as better than the suffering he was enduring in his last years, as a relief and, therefore, for the best. Although she had loved Roy and cared for him almost to the exclusion of all else in his last years, Betty was a *strong woman* with a *strong personal faith* and a well established *network of support* in her church community. She says she never felt alone before Roy's death and continued with that belief afterwards. "I have a spiritual link which gives me peace." Her story of the footprints in the snow tell it all. She had no fear, trusted in God to protect her, said a prayer and went back to sleep! Betty's *personal strength* coupled with her unwavering *faith* provided her with a powerful resource in grief. She mourned but with a calm serenity. She never lost sight of her own value, continued to *nurture herself and others* as she had always done before.

Now Betty's faith remains her quiet companion. She continues to go to church, to work in the church, to attend retreats with church people and to participate in a prayer group. The fact that Betty is the bible study group's oldest member doesn't seem to make any difference at all. At home, Betty cares for herself by *exercising, eating well, reading* and *writing*. She knows what is important to her and lives by it. She continues to find meaning in her life by *helping others*, as she has always done. This work includes hospital auxiliary work, caring for shut-ins, visiting for her church and making quilts for the Scott Mission in Toronto. "When Roy died twenty years ago the centre of my energies went into doing something for others." Being a determined woman with good health and a strong faith have been her chief assets. Together these resources have allowed Betty to face loss with serenity.

"I'm most uninteresting. I've done nothing spectacular in my life." Betty said these words to me as I was talking to her about her life in preparation for this chapter. She has only a grade eight education and that bothered her too, when I approached her to share in this project.

I cannot agree with her that her life has been uninteresting. On the contrary I see her as a woman who has done in her life something which most modern women covet, but have not found easy to attain. Betty has managed to combine a productive career and family life within forty-seven years of marriage, throughout which she maintained her own identity and purpose. Husband and wife in this team were two individuals, each fulfilled in him/herself, living together, giving and taking, interdependent yet fully *independent* too. When Roy was ill Betty cared for him to the exclusion of many things in her life. When he died she began to care for others almost without skipping a beat: without soul searching, brow beating or self-pity. She was able to do that because first and foremost, she had always valued and cared for herself.

Now eighty-eight, Betty is mentally alert and physically very active although this year she decided to give up driving. She has just returned from a visit to family in Boston where her daughter is professor of anesthesiology and pharmacology at the Massachusetts Medical School. She *thinks young*, an asset for us in living at any age. "Occasionally I worry about what will happen to me when I get old," she muses. But she is not old yet! On my last visit to northern Ontario to see Betty this fall, we went to church, drove through the beautiful fall Muskoka colours and ate Thanksgiving dinner out. I marvelled then at her radiant beauty, her ability always to look elegant and be gracious! In particular, I marvel at her strong faith, her will to live a full and selfless life "just one day at a time" and her belief in a personal God who has been at her side, all the days of her life.

3

Louise

out of a glass bubble

beginning comments

After my husband died, like all widows, I had many practical problems to overcome. Because in our partnership I had handled only the usual wifely duties, I found many of my new responsibilities threatening. Business, taxes, car and house maintenance now were all mine to organize. I definitely had no aptitude for money management or auto mechanics or carpentry. But tackling these was not my greatest challenge as I faced life suddenly alone. That challenge would be my children.

At the time of Bob's death my oldest son was fourteen, my daughter twelve, my second son eleven and my little girl just five. At first things went relatively smoothly, partly because we were all in shock and for a time we interacted according to the old way. Eventually, though, both the children and I began to feel our loss. We became emotional powder kegs ready to explode.

At that time I noticed a poster advertising a conference *Helping Children Cope with Death* on our staff room bulletin board. I needed that conference and I went. There, for the first time since Bob's death, I was with people who could talk without fear about death and dying. It was there that I met Louise.

Louise, who was leading a seminar on teenagers and grief, had experienced the sudden death of a relatively young husband, had raised three teenagers alone over difficult times and had initiated many bereavement counselling schemes in her community.

When I spoke to Louise privately after the session, I told her about my situation. Somehow it was very important for me to link myself with someone who had come through the worst with her children and who had not only succeeded with them, but had also grown personally in addition to that success. Louise's success with her children would encourage me to believe in the possibility of my succeeding with my own four children.

A year and a half later when I decided to write this book, I thought immediately of Louise. I asked her to become my first widowhood model. She agreed.

In my interviews with her I discovered that the main challenge in her widowhood had been the loneliness and isolation she felt after Keith died. By having the courage to seek help for herself she inadvertently initiated a bereavement support group model which would become the pattern for other programs in Canada and in the U.S.

LOUISE

I met Keith at a school dance when I was a high school student and he was in accounting. I found him really attractive; handsome, fair haired, blue eyed. He was clever, relaxed, enjoyed reading and sports and fixing things — he was an all round great guy. We dated for five years, then married and had our family, two girls and a boy. Married life was wonderful.

We lived in a newer subdivision. While the children were smaller, I was neighbourly with other young wives and mothers raising their children. Keith was the husband and protector. I nestled into that supportive atmosphere as wife and mother.

I had achieved my goals in life, had completed my education, been married to a good man, had a family. I was perfectly happy.

I began to re-think my priorities after about fifteen years. When the children were babies I wanted to be at home but after that stage passed I didn't want to be running around the neighbourhood drinking cups of coffee and chit-chatting.

So when our youngest, Pam, was eleven, I decided to return to nursing part-time in a medical clinic. Life was busy but I was exactly where I wanted to be. 'I had it all.'

Then, the tornado.

Keith and I were curling together in the Chrysler Bonspiel. When the tornado struck the curling club building, Keith was at the west end skipping and I was at the east. Ambulances rushed us to hospital. My injuries were relatively minor. Keith's were fatal.

That accident has completely changed my life.

At the hospital when they told me Keith had died I didn't

fully understand. I heard but the words didn't get past my ears. I did not believe it. I was numb, very much in shock, not in any way prepared.

I left the hospital that night with a wheel chair, crutches and pain pills. I needed a lot more assistance than that.

At home there were the children to tell and funeral arrangements to make. I was in shock and pain but I carried on with help from many people. I couldn't have managed without my neighbours and friends. They cared for me very well. All my meals were prepared for me. I just sat back quite calmly and enjoyed the food. I remember the funeral home, the long and tedious day of the funeral and hobbling around on my crutches, being with people.

It was not until after the funeral when everyone left that I began to comprehend the truth. Something terrible had really happened and it had happened to us.

A week after Keith's death I felt I had to get back to normal so I decided to return to work. Working was crucial to my survival although economically we were all right.

So I returned to the clinic. I struggled desperately to carry on, somehow managed with the house and finances and children. But the constant emotional and physical pain I felt was totally consuming.

I didn't face reality well. I talked myself into believing that it was only a bad dream, that it would end.

It didn't end. It just got bleaker and bleaker as the months went by. Six months later I was probably worse, more depressed because I realized that this was not a dream. This really did happen. I had to face it.

While I was in this emotional turmoil my health was deteriorating. Scar tissue forming where cement pellets had punctured my back during the collapse of the arena gave me a lot of pain. I had a torn leg ligament too. I lost weight. I looked older. I didn't eat or sleep. In a way it was a blessing that I had the injuries. They forced me to pay attention to my health.

I was forty-one when my husband died. I didn't feel old. Lots

37

of times I felt tired and weary. On the day of the tornado my hair was almost black. Yet when I looked in the mirror I saw a white haired lady. I had to do something about it. I'm blond today because of this.

I also felt so isolated and misunderstood. People didn't know what it was like to have three children and to be widowed. I couldn't share my feelings with anyone. Consequently, I internalized a lot of strong emotions. I joked about my hair, that this was how these feelings were coming out. Some joke!

In order to share my grief with others I began to meet with the survivors of the arena disaster. For awhile it was a help. But we found that while we were together we became totally immersed in going over the events of the evening of the tornado. That's all we ever did. There was no recovery taking place. We just had to stop getting together.

I became very angry with the world. I couldn't believe that they would have a strawberry social at our church when my husband had just died! I wanted the world to stop, to mourn with me. I felt like shrieking 'My husband is dead!'

About this time I had to do a lot of work with my minister. I rejected God; some days I was super angry with Him. At times I believed that there was no God.

My faith has grown out of examining what my feelings were then. It is much stronger now. What I did discover through my grieving and recovering was that I had a personal inner strength quite separate from 'religion.' There was something deep down inside me that gave me strength. Having a sense of that strength was all I needed to know that I would make it.

But that strength certainly took its time arriving. I became abnormally anxious soon after Keith's death about things which had never troubled me before. When my husband was alive I felt protected. I had never had a sleepless night. Suddenly when I was alone, I knew that I was the only one responsible for all of us. I feared for the safety of my children.

To ward off burglars I bought some floodlights and had my son put the lights around the front and sides of the house. Only then could I sleep.

Since we lived in a subdivision where the houses were very close together these lights kept my neighbours awake. They began coming to me and saying they couldn't sleep. We laughed about it and the children and I laughed together. This broke the tension. I was still in deep mourning but I could laugh about myself. It was a good feeling!

It took me about two years to realize that everything was my responsibility now. I had to organize it all: children, bills, cooking, work. I had to learn in my recovery that I couldn't change completely in one day. I could only do one thing at a time. And some things I had to learn about that I never wanted to do. Income tax for instance: I put it off and put it off until the last hour. I got a lot of good advice. Not professional or legal advice although I needed that too. But help from friends who just needed to be asked. By mastering tasks which I had never expected to do and by having the courage to ask for help I was learning and growing.

However, other activities which I had always loved and did well became burdensome. Cooking and eating fell into this category. Cooking was no longer fun. Meals were the pits for awhile. They were junk food out at a restaurant, in front of the T.V., any place that was distracting. We went out to eat a lot.

I think that I dreaded the family meal hour so much because it emphasized that I was now a single mother of a fatherless family. I hated that reality.

I also felt very much ostracized by our couple friends. I didn't feel like going out right away but there was a time when I could see the bridge club that we were in, and the curling club — they were still carrying on with all those activities. I wasn't invited anymore. It felt very lonely to be isolated. I was very much in that fifth wheel syndrome with no social life. I wanted to be included but I had no partner.

Yet when the issue of partners was pushed by a well meaning friend, I balked. About eight months after Keith's death, this friend said that eight months was long enough. Forget about Keith, go to a singles group, meet somebody. I ended up in tears, and my oldest daughter finally stood up and screamed, 'Leave my mother alone!'

I know that my friend did this because she wanted to help. But I was not ready. After my husband's death my sexuality ended. I was not interested in the opposite sex. I was not open to any kind of relationship. I was shocked when men would ask me for a date.

Too many times, too, I was told that I'd get married again. It bothered me that people wanted to matchmake. They think that the way to repair you is to get you linked up with somebody, anybody. I wanted to make the first move if I wanted that. I never did, but I didn't want someone else to set that up for me.

What I needed desperately was a lot of positive support from the people around me, from family and friends both, as I recovered. Hugs. In particular I needed others to accept me as I was without judgment or fear, tears and emotional outbursts and all.

I had a lot of strong emotions during this time because it was a very scary road ahead for me. Being in a grocery store at Christmas time, hearing a song and welling up in tears, seeing Christmas decorations really upset me. Silly. Yes. But having someone to talk to about it, having them say it's not silly was really important.

For me working through grief was like moving one step forward, two steps back. I was often devastated by unexpected emotional pain.

About a year and one half after Keith's death I became desperately lonely. I knew I could be totally frank with my minister so I visited him. Angry and upset I confronted him with my feelings. I told him that it was his responsibility to do something about me. I said I was VERY unhappy. I had no social life. People treated me like I was a little lady in a glass bubble. My neighbours were protecting me to the point where I was just over-saturated with their caring. I had friends who didn't relate to me anymore, who didn't know how to talk to me, were ignoring me. What could he do about me?

He took my outburst seriously. He suggested I needed to find other people in the same situation with whom to share my deepest feelings. Why not organize a meeting?

He was right of course, but I denied it. I didn't know any such people. I was totally depressed, overdone. I had no energy. I didn't care what happened. You wouldn't believe it now to look at me but I was just skin and bones then. I couldn't cope with the idea of organizing people.

After a couple of weeks and continued desperation I gave in and decided I had to try something. Things couldn't be worse. Together we agreed to organize a meeting for widows and widowers at our church. On the appointed night we made coffee for about twenty people and waited. That night one hundred and forty-four men and women attended. They came from Windsor and Essex County, but also from London, Chatham, Thamesford, even from Michigan. Obviously, there were others like me out there.

We continued to hold meetings weekly. I became totally involved with the people I met at group. I needed them and wanted to share with them. I knew that I was supposed to be helping them but they were helping me. I lost interest in my job and instead spent all my time recruiting new support group members, listening to bereaved people and planning our weekly meetings. I decided to quit my job and do this full time — without pay.

I had learned something new about myself then. I learned that I was an impulsive person. This was something I HAD to do and I did it.

Eventually I would find that this commitment to helping bereaved people would become my life's work. But even in this task I had moments of feeling inadequate and guilty. I wondered if I were making too much of my grief. Was I really helping others or just myself? I thought, 'My God, Keith had to die in order for this support group work to happen.' It felt as if I were using his death. But with support from friends and colleagues I became more self-confident about myself and my work.

Finding inner strength and peace of mind took a long time. First I had to go through fears about facing the first anniversary, first Christmas, first Valentine's day, first Easter, first Thanksgiving alone. I braced myself for this first year. But when I passed that milestone I realized that my particular aloneness never passes. I would always have days that were difficult. But I knew I could accept that.

When I went into the hospital for minor surgery three and one half years after Keith's death I had to remove my wedding rings. Getting ready to leave after the operation as I was about to put my rings back on I realized that I was no longer Keith's wife. It was no longer necessary to wear the symbols of our marriage. The world could know, because I had accepted the fact, that I was alone. I had accepted my widowhood. The rings stayed off!

All the time I was struggling with my own recovery, my children had problems too. My two girls and a boy all had horrendous experiences. My son, Wayne, had the worst time because of the social pressures of being the only boy. So the messages to him were to be strong for his mother. Be the man of the house, do all the chores, look after your sisters, get good grades, be strong, don't cry. He believed it all. He had a terrible time for two years. I never did see him cry.

I know that my work with bereaved people helped my family. The children knew about the group, heard me talking openly about death, grieving and feelings to others and eventually my children opened up about their own feelings. We talked about dying and surviving the loss of a loved one together. It was a healthy part of their recovery.

Eventually, the Windsor Mental Health Society asked me to research and report on the status of bereavement resource facilities in our community for them. In my investigation I discovered a definite need for such a support system. To my surprise, I found that doctors, nurses, social workers and therapists — the very people who were constantly dealing with the bereaved — had little, or no training in bereavement counselling. They were virtually unaware of the positive therapeutic value which support groups offered.

The result of this work was that the Mental Health Society accepted my report and decided to initiate a primary preventative bereavement support program in Windsor, the first in the province. I became its coordinator. That was thirteen years ago. I am now still doing the work that I initiated because of Keith's death.

In the course of my work I have done some things which I never dreamed I could do. I have organized meetings, found speakers, produced resource material, spoken to large groups and written papers about my work. I have counselled individuals and large groups. I have grown because of my work. Out of the sharing process I have seen so many positive results for the bereaved.

Over the past thirteen years I have done some real soul searching about the grief recovery process. I have read all the grief books and the research. I have listened to Dr. Kubler-Ross. I have my own thoughts about grief work. It is very painful. It must be done slowly. It may be made easier with the help of books or of a trusted friend, in small or large groups. But the loss *must* be faced. No one can take away the pain. It is like an open, gaping wound; it will bleed. At some point there will be a healing. After the healing process it is possible to become a stronger person.

As for me, I know that out of tragedy came my life's work. When I look back on my counselling the bereaved I realize that I have loved my work. It has been revitalizing, rejuvenating for me.

concluding comments

Louise's husband died seventeen years ago. She accomplished a lot both personally and professionally after Keith's death and found strength to do so in several sources. First, she was not afraid to **speak out** about what she was feeling during the worst part of her widowhood experience. She yelled at her minister, blamed him even, for her woes: — people were treating her "like a little lady in a glass bubble," over-saturating her with their caring. She wanted him to do something. He did. He invited her to *do something*. She did. He suggested that Louise get others together to share their experiences of losing a spouse with her years before the support group movement even began. Louise found many people who felt this need. She got caught up in *a cause bigger* than herself and through it found her own salvation. "This was something I HAD to do and I did it," she explains in her story. She pioneered the *bereavement support* idea in Windsor, helped other communities initiate similar projects, gathered and wrote resource materials and spoke at conferences like the one in London where we first met. By *sharing* with others she *healed herself*. By healing others she got beyond the pain of Keith's death. She learned something about herself in the process.

> I was an impulsive person. . . . I have loved my work. It continues to be revitalizing, rejuvenating for me.

At first, Louise did not find faith in God a resource. In fact she was angry with Him. "I rejected God; some days I was super angry with Him. At times I believed that there was no God." But she worked this anger through with *her minister*; her faith grew out of her questioning and examining process. She also discovered that she possessed an *inner strength* quite separate from religion. "There was something deep down inside myself that gave me strength." *Listening to herself*, acting from that strong place, led her to acknowledge and utilize her unique power in the world, a talent for helping others through pain.

On a cold January day I reconnected with Louise in Windsor where I joined her and many supporters at her book launching. Louise has co-authored a grief counselling book called *Where's Linda?* with a friend. At this celebration, Louise spoke with great pride and excitement about becoming an author. The moment was electrifying! Later Louise brought me up-to-date on her activities in the years since we first met. In 1988 she moved out of Bereavement Resources work for the Windsor-Essex Mental Health into administration work for them as Manager of Special Services. In this new capacity she can utilize the many skills developed over the years in bereavement service while at the same time expanding and innovating in other areas. "A personal challenge moving into management at my age," she reflects.

But it is not necessarily in the area of her work that Louise feels the greatest sense of accomplishment. One source of her pride rests in the fact that all three of her children have university educations and are now successfully on their own. This is a real accomplishment for a widowed mom left to raise a young family alone. And perhaps to be celebrated just as fully, Louise recognizes, is the discovery of the inner strength she found to pull it all together, to conquer her own weaknesses as she faced all the challenges that surfaced after the death of a husband. Now with the children away, work exciting, colleagues, friends and family close, she can just "enjoy."

4

Debby

tossing her hat in the air

beginning comments

When I arrived in London to begin my "new" life a few close friends here knew of my interest in widows and their grief recovery. I met Debby through one of these mutual friends and arranged an interview with her to see if she would share her widowhood experiences with me. As I approached her condominium that night for the interview I wondered what would happen. I knew that her husband, John, had killed himself unexpectedly about seven years ago and that it had been a struggle for her to make ends meet and raise their children on her own. When John died, Deb and her husband were both very young — early thirties — and had three children, all girls aged nine, eleven and fourteen. Deb had absolutely no warning about John's suicidal tendency which surprised me. I thought one would always know, somehow, about something like that.

Would she want to talk about John's death? We sat down over tea and began. Immediately I felt a bond between us perhaps just because we had both been to the same terrible place, widowed young and left quite unprepared to raise our growing children alone. There was no hesitation with Deb. We talked literally for hours and as we did I realized that we had lived through many parallel experiences. We laughed over our fears of leading a manless existence, cried together unexpectedly as we returned to some very deep dark moments in our own grief. We related effortlessly because we had both "been there."

I liked Deb. I found her open, honest, resourceful, bubbly; a really funny lady. After our first meeting we continued to talk over tea or coffee or on the phone when the logistics of our hectic lives made it impossible to meet. We boosted each other, it seemed. At the end of one call Deb told me that she wanted me to read something that she had written. One day soon after that conversation she left a couple of beaten up notebooks, one wire ringed yellow Hilroy binder and one 1979 ONKYO diary between my front doors together with a letter explaining why she wanted me to look at them. She had given me her personal notes in which she had expressed all her feelings about John's suicide and her own struggle to survive that ordeal without falling apart.

That night I read her journals unable to stop, incredulous that she would share such depths of herself with me, a person who had been a stranger to her only a few weeks before. When I finished reading I knew that Deb's story had to be told and that it must include some of her journal entries. Journal writing had kept her sane, helped her heal, shown her herself and allowed her to witness herself change and grow.

The dilemma for me then was obvious. I knew that up until now Deb had not confided in anyone other than the closest members of her family and friends about her husband's suicide. She told me how she often manoeuvered around the truth with people.

Could I ask her to share her story with others when revealing the truth up to this point had been too painful? Would she allow that kind of invasion of her privacy? I asked. She consented almost immediately out of a deep desire to help other widowed women, in particular women widowed because of suicide, through their grief. As she said in her letter left for me with her journals:

> Did you ever in a million years think that you could survive that awful pain? Why did it have to take five and one half years? Surely one should be able to heal just a bit faster. Too bad we couldn't invent a pill!

We couldn't invent that pill, Deb and I. But Deb's story and her diary entries have been better than any pill for me. Deb's story follows. Perhaps you will agree with me.

DEBBY

> Your husband died? He was so young. He was in such good shape. How terrible. How did it happen?
>
> An acquaintance

> It was a heart attack, I would lie. There's no way I will admit to a stranger that my husband killed himself.
>
> Debby

There was absolutely no warning. On a hot night, June 9th, when I woke up about 2:00 a.m. John was standing at the end of the bed, fully dressed, shoes on and restless. He was going for a walk. I was not surprised. It was sultry. I sat up, took his hand, said, 'Have a good walk; see you in the morning,' waved good-bye and went back to sleep. I had no idea that this would be our last time together.

When I woke up Tuesday morning I heard the shower running and assumed that John was getting ready for work. In fact, it was our daughter Cory, not John, in the master bathroom. No car was in the driveway either, but I thought 'Okay John's gone to work early.' He was always the one who opened up mornings.

Once the girls were off to school I called the office to say good morning to him. No answer. Again I thought 'Well, he's probably just out for a coffee.'

I called again at 9:30, this time reaching Steve, John's partner. John was not at work. I began to feel uneasy. One hour later when I called again and John was still not in I was worried. Something was wrong. Steve and I decided to check with the police and hospitals. But there was no information there either.

Around noon as I was making lunch for my girls I looked outside and noticed a brown wagon pulling into the driveway. I thought 'John's ill; Steve's bringing him home.' I felt momentary relief.

Then the car door opened and a police officer and my Doctor got out. They started walking towards the house. I went to the front door and opened it and looked at the Doctor and I knew. I said, 'Oh no.'

He said, 'Yes.'

The girls came to the door to see what was happening. The Doctor said, 'Your father's dead.' Nothing else but 'Your father's dead.'

John had it all planned — carbon monoxide poisoning in the car far away from home and a curt, wounding suicide note which explained nothing, gave me no assurance that at least I had been loved. All John said was 'You will be better off without me.'

I wasn't interested in observing the 'niceties' under the circumstances as far as funeral arrangements went. I wanted no fuss, no funeral, no flowers, no visitation. Nothing. Nobody was going to see John. But when my minister pointed out that John hadn't said good-bye to anyone I changed my mind. I began to plan for a regular funeral.

Steve was a great help. I had no relatives close by. Funny things happened. I remember Steve and I meeting the funeral director. He was this balding little guy who was just a hoot. The first thing he said to me was 'Well I washed your husband's hair today. Your husband sure has a lovely head of hair.' Steve and I just looked at each other. I remember thinking, 'A lot of good it's doing John now! Who gives a damn? I wonder if he noticed John's beautiful blue eyes too?'

And choosing the casket? Some of them were terrible. They looked just like egg crates. These guys were urging me to buy one for three thousand dollars and I didn't have a cent.

I said, 'Now look guys, I have to have something classy but cheap. It's only going to be burned anyway.' So we picked out a fifteen hundred dollar casket with brass knobs.

'You'll look good in that, dear,' I thought.

It seemed that each of my children needed something tangible to keep as a memento of their Dad. So did I. Before John was buried each girl took one of her Dad's rings. Erica took his favourite and wore it on a chain, played with it until it finally wore through and broke. The minute John died I started using his toothbrush — isn't that gross? Erica and I still wear his housecoats; I keep an old sweater of his in my bottom drawer, his aftershave, his powder, his shoe kit and his jewelry box.

At the funeral I was terrified of showing my emotions. When someone touched me during the service I thought 'Get off of me; don't touch me; if you touch me I'll fall apart.'

And when they said, 'Ashes to ashes, dust to dust,' my shoulders started to shake and I thought, 'Please God let me get through this day.' Somehow I found the strength.

Months later on a public bus I saw an old couple sitting

together and I just started to bawl. But other than that no one has ever seen me cry. I do my crying alone.

I was confused and angry with no income and few resources. I had to get my emotions out somehow so I began writing this journal.

Saturday, June 27, 1981   *2.5 WEEKS*
                                        AFTER JOHN'S DEATH

Mom went home to Calgary today and all of a sudden reality has set in. I knew it had to happen but it's always nice to think you can put if off for awhile.

The last few weeks have been so busy. Another way of avoiding the issue. Sometimes I'd like to run away and pretend it never happened. It's really too real though. I never knew one could handle such incredible pain and I wonder if it will ever go away. Friends all tell me that time is a great healer but then again none of them has ever gone through it. I feel that they are all sitting back just watching me — maybe waiting for me to break. If they only knew that I break every second of the day. There isn't a time when I don't think of John. It's so hard to believe that this is really happening. He was (is) my life. I'm sure that there isn't a greater love than I feel for him.

Why? I can't begin to know what pain he must have gone through. Physically, yes, but the mental anguish must have been unbelievable for him to have ended it all. I always thought my love for him could have brought him through almost anything. He must have known how much I loved him.

I wish I knew what it was that made him have to do this. What was the final thing that made his life here so unbearable? I'll never know.

Yes, it was financial and yes, he backed himself into a corner. He had a self-imposed image to live up to and it all came crashing down on him. Why didn't he know that I would have been here to help no matter what? I guess he felt that he couldn't admit failure even to me — the one who loved him more than life itself. He must have believed that I'd be better off without him. Those were basically his last thoughts according to the (suicide) note.

Oh John, why didn't you think further than that? To live without you is to live without happiness, love, sunshine and purpose. I want and need you so badly — just a touch of your beautiful hands or a look of love from your beautiful eyes. How can I ever forget what your arms around me felt like? It seems years since I last felt your arms and yet it is only less than three weeks ago. God, I never ever want to forget what it was like to be loved by you.

Sunday, June 28, 1981

Our daughter is so mixed up. God, if only I could take away some of the pain. Cory loved you so much. My heart breaks watching her sorrow. They all grieve. I wonder if you knew how much they worshipped their Daddy?

I am changing every day. I am so scared of the future. Night time is the hardest. I feel so alone. There's that ache again — it never goes away. I love to talk about you. Right now it's so fresh and the wounds are so raw. It brings you closer if I can say your name.

I want you to be proud of me. And I forgive you. I hope that where you are there is no pain, no tears.

I'm not really strong. I was never too much of a believer but this whole nightmare has shown me there is a God.

I'm very tired right now. It's amazing that I can even sleep at night but you know me. I've always been able to eat and sleep!!

Monday, June 29, 1981

The phone isn't ringing now. I guess life goes on but I almost feel resentful that people have more to do than think of you.

Sometimes I feel that going on is useless; there's nothing to look forward to without you here. No one can ever love or accept me the way you did. I don't want anyone else. The children do keep me going. I do love them.

Tuesday, June 30, 1981   *3 WEEKS AFTER*

I'm exhausted, totally beat. I never wanted to work for a living. I was perfectly content to be your wife. The thought of working all my life is not nice and I am really feeling resentful right now. I guess that's normal.

Driving home today after a twelve hour day I felt so unhappy. I had no one to unwind with, no one to hold me and love me.

I had a nightmare last night. I dreamed you were going to blow your head off and I was packing everything up to leave you, just to run as far away as I could.

Thursday, June 31, 1981

There is so much to do I feel like my head is going to burst open.

You really left me in a bloody mess and right now that makes me very angry. I hate it when this anger comes up. I just can't deal with it. I just want to love you.

Have I been cheated! That makes me mad. I hope these feelings end soon because I don't like them. I understand that they are normal, but I don't like them.

Saturday, July 4, 1981

Guess what? I have laryngitis. Can you imagine — me — not able to talk?

I'm seeing a social worker on Thursday as I feel that the kids really need some help — doesn't everyone in these situations? I'm totally drained right now. No wonder I'm sick.

I'm alone tonight but I guess I might as well get used to it. This is what Saturday nights are going to be for a long time to come.

I wish I could be happy. I can't imagine living with pain like this for the rest of my life. I wonder if anyone ever died from emotional pain? Right this minute I wish I could die.

I eat and sleep because I have to and the children are cared for because I am their mother but the rest of me is completely and totally dead.

I resent every happy couple around me. I remember that not long ago we had, or thought we had, happiness.

Sunday, July 5, 1981

It's kind of like you're in Chicago or Toronto except you're not coming back.

I'm not sleeping very well. I think the pain and sadness is getting worse instead of better.

Your tomatoes are growing. Boy, you're going to miss all the rewards from the garden; I guess you knew that when you planted it though. That must have been difficult for you. I guess near the end everything was difficult though.

A month tomorrow and yet it seems like a hundred years ago. The pain is no less. Time. I can only hope that it heals. Right now it is my enemy.

Wednesday, July 8, 1981   *1 MONTH AFTER*

I'm writing this at Kris' ball game. I had my thing with the counsellor. I guess I'm doing all the right things and really hanging in there. The kids see her next Tues. I want to be sure they are O.K. and I hope they'll open up to her.

Kris won her ball game 21-19.

Sunday, July 12, 1981

Your friend gave me a job. He swore up and down that he needed someone but I think he just gave me the job for us. I am making $175.00 a week. My worry, of course, is how do I support this family? I can't. There is no way. I'm much too frightened to even think about the future. I can't stress enough how scared I actually feel. It's pretty difficult to look upon this as a challenge.

Monday, July 13, 1981

I'm so tired. My body aches but my mind won't turn off to sleep. There's always so much to do.

I'm bitchy right now. I have no patience with the kids and I feel totally defeated. I guess you felt defeated too. I'm on the verge of tears but if I let go I don't think I'll stop for a year.

I have to call someone just to get my mind off my problems. I really hate depending on my friends so much. I like to think I can cope all by myself.

Wednesday, July 15, 1981   *5 WEEKS AFTER*
The girls have seen the counsellor. She seems to think that they are dealing with things pretty well. Erica was afraid I would take my life too. She must have been scared silly. Kris is very envious of any happy family — can't blame her for that as I am too.

Friday, July 17, 1981
Erica is out west right now. Kris and Cory aren't home tonight. They're sleeping over and I'm all alone. I feel very uneasy and very, very lonely.

Monday, July 20, 1981
Today everything seemed to go wrong. Kris started day camp and missed the bus — my fault. Mother is upset with me. I told her not to come and visit and of course she got hurt but I'm not ready for her and the prying that I know she'll do. I knew this would happen. Erica is being very difficult. When all these problems come up I get very angry with you; after all it is all your fault. I'm very frustrated. I still can't deal with the anger.

I start a new job tomorrow. I'm nervous as hell. I have a lot to handle — quite a lot of challenges out there. I don't know how one person can handle it all but I guess now we'll find out just what I'm made of, won't we?

Wednesday, July 22, 1981   *6 WEEKS AFTER*
Yesterday was my first work day. Other than feeling totally exhausted I also felt totally stupid. I'm sure Brian told me how to do things about 50 times and I still didn't know what I was doing. Working for a living is not my cup of tea! But I'd best get used to it and quickly.

Today working seemed to go a bit better. I actually managed to balance the books and get a few things done besides.

There were a few personal problems at the bank today. I have that defeated feeling again. I honestly thought I'd fall apart and cry in the office but managed to keep myself together. What's the point of crying? It can't make any difference. I've never felt quite this depressed before. God, how I hope something positive happens soon.

Life is really strange right now — up at 6:30, work, home, make lunches, tidy up, bed and then up at 6:30 again. Somehow this isn't my idea of living. What the hell is the point to it all? God, I've never felt so miserable.

Kris' team is winning 8-0. They won.

Sunday, July 26, 1981

I can't stand coming home to a place where there are no arms to hold me and no you to comfort me. I need so much to be loved and to be held and to be told that I'm needed. I thought I had all that. I did have all that. How unfair that I don't have it anymore.

This is not living it is merely existing and I hate it with a passion.

Saturday, August 8, 1981   *2 MONTHS AFTER*

I can't believe that it's been since July 26 that I've written in here. I've been so busy and dog tired.

Sat. night and nothing is happening. Sat. was always special for me. It was our night to do whatever we wished. I loved to spend it doing something with friends. I always pushed that. You loved being alone with yourself and I was the one who needed friends around. Now look at me — totally alone and I hate that. I'm almost afraid to be alone with myself as that's when I usually end up in a billion tears. I know I'm feeling sorry for myself.

I hate my job. I seem to have acquired a terrible neck and shoulder pain from doing books eight hours a day. It really is very painful.

I seem to fall apart totally at least once a week. More than anything I need someone to hold me and let me know that I'm still a person. I don't want anything sexual. I'm not ready for that — maybe I never will be. But I do need that warm understanding touch and someone to boost my ego and let me know I'm still worthwhile.

I'm anxious to sell the house now. I hate it in some ways

and yet I hate giving up something I dreamed of having all my life. My dreams are gone.

Sunday, September 13, 1981   *3 MONTHS AFTER*

We certainly have been under quite a strain not only with feelings for you, John, but dealing with Erica and her great temper and anger. Poor Cory and Kris — it's a wonder they still can cope. I sometimes wonder if I'm loosing my few marbles. If this is a test I'm being tested beyond my limit and, God, haven't I passed yet?

Thursday, January 28, 1982   *7.5 MONTHS AFTER*

It's been four months since I've read or written in this book. I've made it through birthdays, Christmas and New Years (not too well but I made it).

I've had my first affair — something that I thought would never happen to me. I can feel you disapproving strongly, John. God, when I found out that a man found me physically attractive and desirable it did something wonderful for me. I was almost used to the loneliness and I almost, I say almost, wish that he had never come into my life — only because it all went bad and now I'm back to square one. I thought it could be something long and lasting and very nice. But instead it has given me so much pain. I thought he might love me like I so need to be loved. No wonder he's running. I probably scare the heck out of him.

I am so confused. Relationships aren't like they used to be when you and I were dating. I don't know what the whole damned world is about today. I was pretty protected when I had you.

I thought I'd cry and think only of you but I didn't. I guess I feel a bit guilty although I know I shouldn't. I was happy for the very first time in six months.

I want to start living again. I want to feel again, laugh again even love again. I think that when I feel, I hurt. You'd think that I'd just shut down and turn off but I don't. I wonder why I don't? Maybe a shrink would have the answer to that one.

Friday, February 12, 1982   *8 MONTHS AFTER*

The kids have been going through their own suffering. Just being twelve is hard enough on Erica but adding to that all that has happened has put her in a spin. I thought she hated me. How was I to know that the reason she was hating me was that she was afraid to love me in case I also took my life?

She has to bowl in a tournament on Sunday and she doesn't want to because you won't be there cheering her on. Naturally the kids think that you didn't love them at all. How can I possibly explain it to them so that they understand why you took your life?

Sometimes I think I have the answers figured out and then sometimes I don't understand your suicide at all.

I feel so tired. I wonder when you're declared medically exhausted? I feel that I'm heading to that point. I seem to do a lot of crying lately and I'm always down. How I wish I could take a week off and just lie in the sun and not think of anything. I never get time for myself. It's just work all the time and then facing the kids and they fight so much.

I am very lonely. I wonder if it ever goes away?

Monday, March 15, 1982   *9 MONTHS AFTER*

If I'm totally exhausted it must be Monday. I'm still just existing, surviving. I wonder what it is that makes some people have that strong survival instinct and others not have it? I guess we survivors just keep hoping that there's something better waiting around the corner. Well world, don't let me down.

Tuesday, April 20, 1982   *10 MONTHS AFTER*

I'm waiting for something, anticipating, but I know nothing is going to happen. Am I waiting for you to come back?

I've also been waiting for the year to be up. I almost expect a reward at the end of it all. When will I ever accept the fact that this is it?

I'm trying to be totally independent. For months I seemed to be looking everywhere for a man but now I don't feel so desperate. I've learned that I can support myself and the kids and I have gotten through a lot of long and lonely nights when

I thought I'd surely die from loneliness and unhappiness. Sometimes I don't even mind having this bed all to myself.

I've taken a giant step putting the house up for sale. I want to start over now. I want to get rid of the memories.

Tuesday, May 20, 1982   *11 MONTHS AFTER*

As I approach May 22 and June 9, I find myself at a breaking point. This Saturday would have been our 17th anniversary. I never in my wildest dreams thought I'd be spending it without you. On June 9th you will have been gone from me a whole year.

Guess what? A blind date. I actually went out on a blind date last month. How awful. I would have enjoyed my own company more. I yawned through the entire movie.

I can never replace you or what we had but it sure would be nice to come close. I sound like I've dated hundreds of men. Wrong! I'm really and truly beginning to think that I must be a real nothing. Nobody, but nobody wants me. What the heck is wrong with ME? I think I have a lot to offer. I try to tell myself that I don't need anyone, that I can make it on my own but somehow I cannot believe that. Loneliness is a terrible thing and I need love.

Everyone tells me how great I'm doing, how strong I am, how they admire me. Shit, I want to scream at them all and tell them exactly what I feel, what I'm going through. God, don't let any of them go through what I'm going through. How I hope I can make it through June 9th in one piece. I just can't fall apart at work. I just can't.

Tuesday, May 25, 1982

On our anniversary my boss and his wife sent me flowers and a card that said, 'To a super receptionist.' I waited seven months to hear that so it was a big lift to the ego.

I've had the house up for sale since March 30th and have been going through hell with the stress of it all. I'm so anxious to make a new start.

A song broke me up the other day. 'The Way We Were.' Music can really get to me more than anything.

I want you back, John. Tomorrow I'll put on my happy face

and once again I'll pretend that everything is fine but, dear God, things aren't fine.

Friday, June 4, 1982   *1 YEAR AFTER*
Thank God there are some good people. I'm rich in friends. Where else would you find a co-worker coming over to your house to plant flowers?
God, I'm dreading the 9th.

Sunday, July 18, 1982   *1 YEAR 1 MONTH AFTER*
Well, I made it through the ninth. I have made it through the year. Somehow I feel that now I can actually go on. I still feel great love for you. I still feel great sadness. I'm stronger and a whole lot wiser.
I've sold the house and bought a condo and, of course, it scares me to death to take such a large step on my own but I have to do that now. It scares me to be spending money on carpets and wallpaper. God, I hope I'm doing the right thing. If I make mistakes I have to pay for that too.
I am pretty brave after all. I do feel pretty proud of myself. I never in a million years thought I could stand on my own. The legs are pretty shaky but I just might be O.K.

November 14, 1982   *1 YEAR 5 MONTHS AFTER*
It's been five months since I last wrote. We've been in the new house three months now. I love this house. The change is really a good thing for me.
Cory turned seventeen yesterday. I was wishing it was seventeen years ago. I was happy and so naive then. Cory's boyfriend was here for dinner. I thought what it would have been like with you here teasing her. I dread to think of the day she marries and she won't have her Daddy walking down the aisle with her.
You know I'm so very jealous of her mainly because she's happy; she has Dan and I don't have anyone.
I wonder if I'll ever feel alive again. I feel the tears just beneath the surface but so many times I can't cry. I'm afraid to cry.
Sometimes I think that I can only be happy if our spirits meet. I would never take my own life but somehow if I were

to die (hopefully peacefully) by God's hand then I must say I wouldn't be unhappy. I feel that it can't be over for you and me because we didn't have enough time.

Sunday, May 8, 1983   *1 YEAR 11 MONTHS AFTER*
Today is Mother's Day. It is also six months since I wrote in here.

Christmas was ridiculous. I was so sick. Cory broke up with Dan. Kris got the flu. It just wasn't a good time.

Erica has put me through a living hell for most of the year but I think its all been a blessing in disguise as she's now getting some long overdue help. God, but you two are so similar it's scary. We've been through so much it's not surprising that one of us has an emotional problem. I hope that in time Erica comes out of it but I have such nagging doubts.

Tuesday, Sept. 20, 1983   *2 YEARS 3 MONTHS AFTER*
I've been fired from my job. I know it wasn't justified.

It's scary not to have an income and no prospects. I'm using this time for me and trying to get me in order. I really need a rest as I didn't take it 2½ years ago. I only hope I can hold on financially.

I got through June 9th again. I finally have time to think and I know that you'll never be here again. The pain seems to be easing somewhat — maybe I'm in remission. I've finally realized that you're dead. I always knew it but I never believed it, I guess. There will always be a sadness and a void but somehow I've accepted that and somehow it makes things a lot easier.

March 26, 1984   *2 YEARS 9 MONTHS AFTER*
Almost nine months have gone by and I'm still not working. I'm pretty angry with myself right now. I'm really starting to panic. I tried to get into a course at the college but there's no way. There aren't any jobs out there that I'm trained for and I don't know what the hell to do. I'm so frightened for my future.

I've been going to Woman Power for counselling. I feel like that's my last hope.

I'm angry at the whole world now. I'm angry at you, John, for screwing up my life so beautifully. I think if you were here right now I would beat the hell out of you. I guess I'm feeling pretty low right now and have a very low opinion of myself. I feel like a number one loser. How can anyone find me desirable if I hate myself so much?

These thoughts are something I would never share with another living soul. I wouldn't want anyone to know how badly I'm feeling about me. Where do I go for help? Where do I go for understanding? I wonder if anyone has ever felt this way?

Friday, January 9, 1987   *5 YEARS 6 MONTHS AFTER*

Dear Peggy,

This journal is for you. Here it is almost three years since I wrote in the silly thing. I have read it all over again and at some points I decided that you'd never see it mainly because it's pretty cornball but then I thought, no, I'm going to let you read it because I know you will understand every word I have written.

I had forgotten a lot of the feelings I had — the anger and the tears — I don't remember a lot about those feelings but they certainly were there — and very strong!

I feel so sad for those who have to go through what we have gone through. I truly do ache for the person I used to be. I guess I had to crawl before I walked. I'm still looking forward to running.

I'm still pretty scared of what the future holds for me. But right now I feel in control and that is a good feeling.

The good thing about having written the things I wrote is the looking back on it all and knowing now just how far I have come along. I still feel a lot of those things but not as strongly as I once felt. Thank God those years have passed and thank God I don't have to live through them again. I honestly don't think I could do it.

I made it through. I really did it! I almost feel elated right now because I survived like I thought I never could survive.

You know maybe there really is a God out there somewhere. Or maybe strength comes from within?

I have met one of my goals. I have survived and I have brought up my children to the best of my ability.

Unlike that other Deb, I don't want to lie down and die anymore. I want to see what is waiting around the next corner.

I didn't like the person who wrote all those things. She is someone I don't even recognize now. This is a big positive, Peg, because I like the person I am now. I'm not afraid; I'm not depressed, I'm not lonely and I'm not scared to be out on my own. I guess time is the big healer.

You know for the first time in a long time I feel like I just might make it and oh, what a good feeling that is — like Mary Tyler Moore tossing her hat in the air!!!

> Love you,
> Deb

concluding comments

I have just re-read Deb's story. It says a number of things very clearly to me. First, Debby is a number one *survivor*, not a loser as she described herself in her journal entry of March 1984. She coped without much external help. She had the *instinct* to do what she needed most for herself — get her *feelings*, fear, anger, frustration, love, hate, despair — *out*. Out for her was on paper in her journals. She found the way that best suited her by *listening to her own inner guide*. Some part of her saw her need and got her *writing*. The survivor, Deb, took over and gave her the *courage* to heal herself.

Secondly, Deb began to see herself as she really was, and to recognize her strengths as well as her blemishes. By the time she wrote her letter to me five years after John's death, she really liked the person she was and celebrated that new woman. "I truly do ache for the person I used to be. I guess I had to

crawl before I walked. I'm still looking forward to running."
By *caring for herself* Deb had less and less need to depend on
caring from the outside. She became self-sufficient and proud
of the fact. She could handle her move, her kids, her finances,
her emotions. And she was damn proud of it. She exhibited
zest and *courage* in her years of doing what had to be done.
I haven't heard too many women describe a funeral director
as honestly and with as much *humour* as Deb when she began
telling her story to me. "He was this balding little guy" made
me laugh when I first heard it and still does! Deb's humour
carried her through some very depressed days after John's
suicide. She had the courage to *make* difficult *changes*, too and
these changes nurtured her. A year after John's death (July 18)
she writes "I sold the house and bought a condo and of course,
it scares me to death to take such a large step on my own but
I have to do that now." Later (November 14) she writes "We've
been in this house three months now. I love this house. The
change is really a good thing for me." Deb also had the courage
to seek *professional help* for her children when she became
worried about their behaviour one month after John's death.
"I'm seeing a *social worker* as I feel the kids really need some
help — doesn't everyone in these situations?" Later she did
the same for herself going to *career counselling* when she lost
her job.

It is scary having no income and no prospects, Deb admitted,
but she decided two years into her widowhood to *invest in herself.*
"I'm using this time for me and trying to get me in order. I
really needed a rest as I didn't take it two and a half years ago."
Deb was *wise* about her own needs. After two years of caring
for everyone else she began to take stock of herself. Making
this decision was a turning point for Deb: the point at which
she stopped, waited, then began to *look forward* with a new
energy and enthusiasm. Up until now she had been totally
exhausted. Now her strength was returning to her. Its source
wasn't clear to Deb, maybe God, she thought, or maybe the
"strength comes from within?" (letter to me January 1987).
Whatever its source, this power altered Deb's *attitude*. Now,

she began to find a new self-confidence, and an indomitable spirit and joy for life again.

As she said in her final letter to me:

> I made it through. I really did! I almost feel elated now because I survived like I never thought I could survive.

As she anticipates the future Deb is a changed person:

> Unlike that other Deb, I don't want to lie down and die anymore. I want to see what is waiting around the next corner.

Deb's life begins again. As she cares for herself, passion returns. No wonder she goes on to meet many of her goals. Her children do well. Deb finds a new man. All of this is built on a strong relationship with herself.

Deb and I had a visit again last night, a sort of pre-publication celebration. I wondered what she considered her best accomplishments now, ten years after John's suicide. First, she is proud of her children. They have all turned out well. She is also proud of the fact that she was able to get through the difficulties of mothering. Krista is now nineteen, Erica twenty-one and Cory twenty-five. This summer Cory was married in a beautiful wedding which Deb planned and executed flawlessly. For many, it was the best wedding they had ever attended.

Deb is very proud of herself and proud of the fact that, through it all, she has not become bitter and has kept her sense of humour. She is involved in a solid relationship with a man who knew John. She had always wondered if she would be happy again, not lonely. Her message:

> It does happen. This man makes me very happy. I've worked hard on this relationship. The outcome is that we can talk about anything.

Deb is at a crossroad in her work. Not happy for years, she just recently left her job and security. As she said to me, "sometimes the hat feels like it's going to fall in a mud puddle." I know Deb better. She confided in me that if she could choose to do anything at all, she would choose counselling work. I suspect that with characteristic good humour and courage, Deb will go for it all.

Seeing Deb again is like a tonic. She remains fun, vibrant, caring and, as she might have observed of someone else, "just a hoot." She is also a very strong women. I want to throw my hat in the air with her!

5

Jane

ashes in a mountain trout stream

beginning comments

As I sit here with the chilling rains outside, I think of how I yearn for spring, for the season which warms the earth and encourages the tender seedlings to flourish. I remember Jane's story, connecting the events of the last few years of her life with my image of spring. After her husband's death she was in a cold winter of grief; through her personal realization and growth work, Jane's winter turned to spring.

In 1958 Jane married a man over twenty years her senior. Together they led a very active life of travel and adventure. Together they had two children. When George became ill suddenly and died, Jane went into a shell. Fortunately her children who were still at home helped. When they left Jane became depressed. She eventually sought help from a qualified therapist and learned that it was not a weakness to do so. Doing her own grief and growth work enabled her to find a new inner strength and to grow as an individual apart from husband and children.

I met Jane when her growing process had just begun. We have discussed the experiences of our widowhood with candour and together we began support groups for widowed women, later for widowed men and women, as a result of our combined learning. The path Jane has taken following George's death has elicited my compassion, my respect and my admiration.

JANE

George and I were married out west in 1958. He was a real 'kindred spirit.' We shared a love of the outdoors, of camping and hiking, and adventure. He was in public relations, a writer, speaker, and a former diplomat, with two sons from his first marriage. We had two children of our own, and eventually moved east because most of our work was there.

George left the large corporation he was with and we started a consulting, lecturing and public relations business together.

George was the speaker and writer of the team. I was the photographer, bookkeeper and travel organizer, and we shared the research. We travelled a great deal in South America, the Indian subcontinent, and across Canada and the U.S.A. and met people from very different backgrounds. As with many independent businesses, financially we had some very good times and some lean ones. I took a part-time job to stabilize our economic situation, mothered the children and complained to my husband about the ordinary daily frustrations, like pipe tobacco on the carpet. Now I wish I'd had the sense to know how unimportant such irritations were. I wish I had spent more time just being with George.

In 1980 we planned a trip to India for a month. In India George wrenched his back, complained of the heat and was tired, which was unlike him. Despite all this, we had a memorable trip and I returned to Canada ahead of George who stayed on to rest. A week later I met him at the airport. The moment I saw him being wheeled from the plane I knew he must be seriously ill.

The next day our family doctor admitted him to hospital. Three days later his illness was diagnosed as terminal cancer. The specialist gave him three days to live. Ironically, that day, the garden which meant so much to George burst into spring with cherry blossoms and tulips. He survived three weeks. On June 4, another beautiful spring day, George died. The whole family was in shock.

We had a memorial service — a celebration of his life — and afterwards, as he had requested, a party at the house where friends related their memories of George. Surprisingly, it felt good. I kept his ashes in a box in the house until we could make a trip west to scatter them as he had wished. Then I went back to work and to the routine with the children and house as usual. But it wasn't 'as usual' ever again.

A death in the family puts a horrendous strain on every member of the family. Rory's 18th birthday was on Father's Day, ten days after George's death. He wrote his grade thirteen finals the same week and didn't do as well as he should have. No one at school thought to suggest that under the circumstances he should be exempt. In July, he had complicated surgery following an accident to his hand. Over the next two years, we all took turns going to the hospital with accidents or health problems. Amanda fell asleep at the wheel of the car — the result of the strain and two part-time jobs. Physically in those early years I had little energy, suffered from stress-related health problems, and frequent migraines, and generally felt tense and down. For short periods of time I would forget my situation, but mostly fear pressed like a heavy weight on my chest. I wasn't used to feeling out of control emotionally and it scared me.

Rory's trip to Australia, in November of the year George died, was difficult for me. Rory missed his family and was very homesick being so far away from us, especially at Christmas time. I missed him even more — no George, no Rory — and worked myself into a state of worry and guilt over this. I felt as if I were in a deep black hole, and I didn't have the energy to climb out. I wasn't coping well with decision-making either. My daughter finally said to me, 'Mother, I am not Dad. You are capable of making a decision yourself.' She urged me to seek outside help.

Finally, I went to a family counsellor who listened and stayed with me while I poured everything out. During the first session he asked me if I felt as though my heart were breaking. I thought he had described it perfectly. My frozen heart felt as if it were cracking in two. He managed to get me to 'thaw' a bit and to accept the fact that I couldn't change some things that were tearing me apart, such as my not being with George when he died and Rory's absence. I had to let go of the guilt and worry over things I could not control. That was my first step.

Although these sessions helped me, I couldn't continue to see a therapist because of the financial strain. So I went back to my former pattern of working hard all day and grieving at night. I was fortunate that I had the children at home for awhile, which kept me on a level course outwardly. The house didn't feel so empty. Then the awful 'someone is always saying goodbye' syndrome began. Every time one of my children left home I went through a feeling of panic. I was so scared of losing one of them. Somehow if they were living at home I felt I could save them if they got hurt. But when they were so far away I felt I had no control over their safety. My guilt over not having noticed George getting so ill made me want to have a second chance to prove that I really could do better. Finally, four years after George's death, when Rory left for Nova Scotia, and Amanda for Vancouver, I had to face the fact that my children would not be living at home ever again. Suddenly I found the empty house desperate.

I was also having a problem adjusting socially to my single state. When I first started mixing with people, I experienced the 'fifth wheel' syndrome I'd heard about. I felt like I was either a nuisance or a threat. I was jealous of those with mates, and angry with anyone who complained about a spouse's faults, but I put on a cheerful face, and acted like a strong, independent woman, even though inside I was crying. I did have friends who were wonderful — those with sensitivity and caring, and those who had been through death or divorce themselves — and I blessed them. But when it really came down to it, they were not family and it was my husband and children that I really wanted with me.

How did I solve the problem of my loneliness? I became a total workaholic. I worked as many evenings as possible, hundreds of hours, just to escape. I hated coming home to the empty, silent house. I wanted to be too tired to think.

Looking back, there was something else that was stopping me from coming to grips with my situation. I still had George's ashes in the house. Finally, the family was able to get together four years after George's death to perform this ritual over a mountain trout stream north of Vancouver — a place where George had fished many times. After that, I felt I was going backwards emotionally. I couldn't seem to pull myself out of feeling low. Work was exhausting and I began to resent it. I wondered whether the rest of my life was going to be like this: slog, slog, slog, and getting nowhere.

Then one weekend while attending a workshop on male-female relations something in me snapped. I began to cry and couldn't stop. Here I was, crying in public when I didn't want anyone to know I was still grieving, and there was nothing I could do about it. I was frightened.

Fortunately the workshop leaders took me home with them and we talked and talked which really helped. They urged me to return to the counsellor I had seen before. They also urged me to attend one of the Shalom retreats I had heard about and resisted as 'not for me, thanks!' But what really made me listen this time was that both of them told me that they had been to several of these retreats and that retreats had helped them get on their feet after personal crises. I was amazed. They didn't seem to be the type of people who would need something like that. They came across as strong and competent — and apparently I did to them. In fact, they had even wondered why I was bothering to attend their workshop because obviously I had my life organized and together! It was a lesson in not judging people externally.

I listened to their experiences and it gave me just the push I needed to ask for help. I felt so out of control that I had nothing to lose. The retreat weekend started in June, by coincidence on the anniversary of George's death. That weekend would change my life. I joined several others in a remote country location. Every one of us had some issue to tackle. Some had the pain of divorce, some wanted to improve relationships with partners, and some had childhood trauma to explore. My work was my grief. The leader built up our trust immediately by having us pledge to stay for the weekend, wish goodwill to every one present, and promise to keep the confidentiality of the personal information shared there. It quickly became a safe place where expressing emotions was acceptable. I began my weekend crying and don't think I stopped for two days!

On that retreat we worked together as a group, writing, storytelling, meditating and dancing. We became support and positive reinforcement for each other. During the weekend each of us also had one individual experiential session with the leader.

My personal time involved psychodrama in which I relived George's death both as it has been and as I would have liked it to be. In that hour I said everything I wished I had had the opportunity to say to him before his death. I needed and felt the support of all my fellow retreat participants during that time. When each of us had finished, we celebrated by playing appropriate music and dancing.

Part of the value of the weekend for me was in doing this concrete grief work. But it had other significance too. For the first time since George's death, I was able to put my own situation in perspective. I learned that some people were only now letting go of events that happened fifteen and twenty years ago! I didn't need to be ashamed of holding in unresolved grief for a mere five years. I stopped judging myself because I knew I wasn't alone. Others healed slowly too. By allowing myself to be just as I was, I took a big step in my own healing process. The level of caring was deep and unconditional there. From that weekend a wonderful period of personal growth began for me.

As part of that growth, I resolved to continue my private therapy sessions. While four years ago I couldn't afford to spend that money on myself, now I realized I couldn't afford not to. I now knew that getting help for myself was an investment in my future. And I was worth it! I had to move out of the 'wife and mother' phase of my life, and into who I really was as an individual. Because I had married very young I had never had time to find this out.

Shortly after the retreat I took some time off to visit Rory in B.C. We went camping together and one day as we walked along the beach some old tensions between us surfaced, and I ended up in tears. Had this happened a year before I would have been really depressed but now I was able to hear the meaning behind his words. Later as we worked together fixing up a log cabin for him, we drifted into conversation about George and the meaning of life and death. Because of my personal work I found I could talk and listen more openly. Because I was trying to set myself free from the past, I was willing to let Rory free himself as well. 'If you love something let it go.' It would be a turning point in our relationship, and I was optimistic we might become friends.

On a Christmas visit with Amanda in England I realized that I couldn't and shouldn't rely on my children. They were well into their own lives. I had to build mine. With that in mind, I started organizing my own trip to the mountains of Nepal, something I had always dreamed of doing. Both my children said, 'Go for it!' By March I had put down a deposit for my first trip alone. In addition I started to develop a network of friends at home, and to organize my life with my own needs in mind. I refused to consider a better job out of town because I knew that friends were more important than money; my friends were here. I became my own priority for the first time in my life. I began to work less, and spent more time cultivating new interests and getting in shape for the trip.

During the preparation for my Nepal trek I did another retreat (my wedding anniversary this time) which focused on the theme of spirituality and sexuality. When I learned that the theme would centre around love and passion I felt resentful, then angry. I was looking for love and not finding it. Love and passion meant relationships and sex to me. I thought I'd come to the wrong retreat. If I hadn't pledged to stay, I would have left. Gradually it became apparent that the weekend's theme did not apply to relationships and sex only. It meant loving oneself, and regaining a passion for life. I totally reversed my negative attitude towards the weekend and made a personal commitment to these two factors. As I explained my trip to my friends on the retreat, I realized that for me Nepal would be much more than a tourist jaunt to some faraway place. It would be a personal pilgrimage to celebrate the beginning of a new life!

I received all kinds of support from friends for my Nepal venture. Some experienced hikers gave me advice and gear so that I would be as well equipped as possible. Others offered support just by understanding the nature of my quest. By the time I boarded the plane I knew I was going to Nepal with the blessings of a dozen friends, and my children as well.

The trip fulfilled all my wildest dreams. I have always loved mountains, and feel a sense of a greater Spirit there. Their everlasting nature put my problems into perspective.

The physical challenge of the trip was tough. I hiked nineteen days to thirteen thousand feet, keeping pace with three male British climbers. We crossed decrepit swinging bridges, negotiated landslide trails barely wide enough for my hiking boot, waded through icy rivers and climbed thousands of rough stone steps to a mountain village. At times I wondered why I had chosen this way to celebrate a new life. But my fears were physical ones, not paralyzing emotional ones, and I could deal with them. I felt truly alive again and full of joy.

Our *sirdar* or leader, Nawang, was a special mentor for me on my pilgrimage. A former Buddhist monk and mountain climber who chanted his prayers on the trail and in his tent each morning, Nawang was in touch with the earth and his soul. He became an inspiration for me. We had many discussions about life and death. The occasional time when I broke down he understood, and although we came from different cultures, we communicated that understanding between us.

There were so many 'miracles' on that trip. Nawang was one. We had fine weather the whole time, a rare thing in mountains anywhere. Our final destination was a holy place of pilgrimage for both Hindus and Buddhists and it seemed right that I should be going there too. The group was small, and the members of it were also searching for new meaning in their lives. I felt I was being given a gift each day.

However, the real miracle was my accident. Early one morning as we started our return journey my foot slipped, and my pointed walking stick went into my right eye. I couldn't see anything, my nose started to bleed and half my face went numb. Swelling and pain mounted, I felt sick and in shock and took the few antibiotics we had in our emergency supplies. There was nothing else to do — no doctor or hospital on the route. So we patched up my eye and I went on, stumbling because

I had lost my depth perception. I would have to 'feel' my way along the rough trail for the rest of the trek. But curiously the panic left me and I felt quite calm. It was almost as if I were being given another test for my new inner strength. Four days later a doctor we met by chance in a group of German trekkers told me the stick had missed the pupil of my eye by half an inch. Miraculously, my vision would return.

Everything came together on that trek — physically, mentally, emotionally, and spiritually. On all those levels I found a new awareness of life and a deeper sense of who I was. It was worth every penny I had saved for it, and every minute of the planning and dreaming.

George always used to say 'Count your blessings — if you have health and friends, you should never complain,' and he was right. In a sense, I have taken up his love of adventure and through it found a way to renew my enthusiasm for life. I have two wonderful supportive children who are also my friends, and they won't let me backtrack. They keep challenging me to 'Go for it!' in all sorts of ways. And I have lots of good friends who care enough to do the same.

My personal growth after George's death didn't start until the fifth year of widowhood. That too has been a long perilous journey but one I do not regret. This seventh year of my widowhood has been very special. Finally I feel that I am a whole person again. I'm already planning my next trip; maybe it will be ocean kayaking this time.

I know I can tackle anything!

concluding comments

As I re-read Jane's story what stands out for me is her *will power*, *physical stamina* and *courage*. She hiked alone in high mountains and in remote places. But before she could utilize all those talents she had to admit her pain and stop repressing her powerful feelings. To do this she had to seek *professional help*. Though she had been conditioned to "go it alone," to be strong and in control, some force deep inside told her that this way was not working. One part of her would not accept that life would remain exhausting; just "slog, slog, slog and getting nowhere." She had to save herself but could not until she broke down publicly, out of control and scared. Her *fear* forced her action; fear became her ally and her teacher. Without it she might not have acted as she did. Fear sent her to a therapist where she began to talk, to share her feelings of anger, guilt and fear. At the *retreats* Jane continued her grief work by reenacting George's death and by being with him, by accepting her aloneness and by discovering her *love for herself* and her *passion for life*.

From the therapy sessions she moved out into the world and did her work externally. She began to let go of George and guilt over the past. *Letting go* of her adult children and standing on her own two feet were part of this work. Then *accepting* her *alone state* and building on it by cultivating new friends, doing things which excited and challenged her such as the Nepal pilgrimage, choosing to pass on a promotion in order to remain in an environment that supported her, all empowered Jane. She was able to make these decisions because she had become more aware of her inner needs. Together with this was a new conviction that she was of *value*. She was a good investment and worth every penny she spent on therapy hours and unusual trips. Finally, Jane's return to the mountains which had always been a source of joy for her reawakened her to her *spirituality*, to a power greater than herself. This trip to Nepal became, as Jane says, "a healing pilgrimage."

First, Jane admitted her vulnerability. Then she found herself.

Then she began to care for herself alone and found joy in her wholeness. As she reconnected with nature and with a greater spirit in the world on her mountain trek, her problems seemed diminished. She writes, "The everlasting nature (of the mountains) soon began to put my problems into perspective."

It was about this time that I met Jane, saw her excitement about her new life and began to work with her. Together we initiated and co-facilitated grief work support groups for widowed men and women. In *helping others* Jane was helping herself. There she affirmed for herself and others that healing takes time — years not months.

Now ten years after George's death, Jane recalls some highlights. The kayaking trip mentioned at the end of Jane's chapter did materialize. Those two weeks of ocean kayaking in the Queen Charlotte Islands were followed the next year by an African adventure in the tropical mountains of Rwanda to see the "gorillas in the mist" and to climb sixteen thousand feet to the top of Mount Kenya. This year in June, Jane joined her son on the tenth anniversary of George's death to hike in the mountains near the stream where his ashes are scattered. In October, Jane joined her daughter in Cambridge, England where Amanda received her doctorate. Another good year, I would say!

Ironically, once Jane had finally found that life alone could be good she met a man who had been on his own too. Now, she is quietly enjoying the opportunity to be with a new partner.

Recently Jane and I discussed how it has taken her far longer than she would have thought possible to deal with her grief and to find joy again. Together we remembered the Chinese ideogram for the word "Crisis," which perfectly describes the dynamics of losing a spouse. This word is made up of two symbols, the one "danger" and the other "opportunity." The crisis of the death of a spouse fits with the ancient Chinese wisdom. It is a dangerous time for a widow. It is also a wonderful opportunity for her to learn to see with new eyes, live life differently and to grow into all that she can be.

Jane found a new sense of self through her physical accomplishments and her supportive relationships. She also learned that she is not just the other half of a lost spouse. She is whole within herself and can bring that wholeness into the relationship with her new partner. Jane longed to be able to feel the joy of spring once again. It is accomplished!

6

Sylvia

the water's fine

beginning comments

Sylvia is a joy to meet. Her home is comfortable, spacious with lovely gardens and reflects her love of art and music. I had not met Sylvia before and wondered if our difference in age would hinder our communicating. I had no need to worry. First Sylvia welcomed me warmly into her kitchen where she had tea and hot buttery muffins already out on the table. We were off to a good start!

Once into conversation it seemed we had much in common. We shared a passion for music, a keen interest in the world around us, in art, books, ideas and people. We found it easy to share our stories despite the generation difference between us. Sylvia was seventy-one and I, forty-two. Sylvia told me her story openly with warmth and good humour but with absolutely no self-pity. Widowed at twenty-nine she remarried a year later.

Sylvia became widowed a second time when she was sixty-seven. She nursed both husbands through long terminal illnesses and recovered herself from a mastectomy which changed her outlook on life. Sylvia works a busy day as music teacher and adjudicator, travels extensively and keeps close ties with friends and family. She is a woman, I discovered, who knows herself well and who lives each moment to the fullest.

Sylvia has much wisdom to communicate to newly widowed women. Her special "no nonsense, go for it all" philosophy comes out of her unique ability to bring to adversity a delightfully positive spirit!

SYLVIA

I have been widowed twice, so mine is quite a story.

When Nat and I were married he was working as a purchasing agent for an engineering firm and I was teaching piano part-time at the Royal Conservatory of Music in Toronto. We had our first child, a girl, Sandi. When Sandi was born Nat decided he wanted another five thousand dollars worth of life insurance and in 1945 five thousand dollars was a lot of money! He passed the severe insurance company tests to get special rates. There was no sign of his illness then.

Six months later I learned that my husband was terminally ill. I didn't know whether it would be six weeks or what. He had a very rare skin disease. No one knew anything about it. I couldn't face telling him. I didn't tell him a lie but I didn't tell him the whole truth either. I said he had a very serious illness and that there really wasn't any treatment. The only thing that could help him would be his will to live.

The hospitals didn't want him because a skin disease of that nature was no fun to nurse. So they sent him home and I made him as comfortable as possible. He wasn't a demanding person all his life but he was demanding in his illness.

I ran the household completely for two years while Nat was ill. I didn't work much during that time but the Toronto Conservatory of Music where I had been teaching piano heard that I was in trouble and offered me full-time teaching when I wanted it. That was very good to know, because the faculty was not hiring at the time. Looking after Nat became a twenty-four hour job and we had a baby in the house too. Thank goodness I was young. I was twenty-nine.

Nice things happened. Friends were just marvelous. They would come over and we would have a regular Red Cross meeting at our house making bandages. Family and friends would take me every evening for a drive to get me out of the house. Some would stay with Sandi and Nat and make the bandages for the next day. I think that's one of the very important things in life, to have that kind of support system.

Nat died one and a half years after his illness was diagnosed. In May Sandi turned two. In October Nat died. I was left a young widow with a two year old child. The next year I spent readjusting. First, I went back to work full-time at the Conservatory. For that, I needed to arrange babysitting. Post war, there were still nursery schools as a part of the public education system originally intended to allow women to work for the war effort. I managed to get Sandi into one and it was perfect for

us but after a few months they did a means test on me and, because I owned a bungalow and a car, Sandi was out. I joined together with other mothers in similar situations to keep the school open for us but it didn't work. That was my first introduction to child care problems. I had to find a school for Sandi. The only all day one I unearthed was called Hillcrest. I couldn't afford it so I bartered for it. I became its music director and Sandi became a student there. To help in the house, I found a bible college student who needed a home and a little spending money. I took Sandi to school and Betty picked her up, looked after the house until I got home and had dinner ready for us. I couldn't afford to pay her much.

I certainly had to work very hard to pay the bills. I can remember saying to Betty, 'Look money is short this week. We have eleven dollars for the table. I don't care if we have to eat spaghetti all week, it will have to do.' and it did and it wasn't the end of the world. Those things didn't really matter. Sandi and I had good times together for cheap. We'd go down to Union Station and watch the trains come in and after, go to the Diana Sweets for an ice cream soda. Those were precious times. You can make do with very little.

There were other problems at the time which were more upsetting for me than the monetary ones. I had tremendous fears. In retrospect those fears were all around being a one parent family and how this would affect Sandi. A favourite uncle became a sort of a father figure to her. We'd go over there once a week for dinner.

And then I went through a period when I started to lose confidence in myself. I began to wonder if I could support this child and myself. And my fear became almost a self-fulfilling prophecy. It was interfering with my teaching.

I had the good sense at the time to tell myself to pull up my britches and do something. I phoned a psychiatrist and told him my problems. I spent six months with him. It was very expensive for me but I used some of my carefully hoarded insurance savings. I could not have afforded him otherwise.

In my first year as a widow, I was always with Sandi when

I wasn't working. I was completely exhausted. I couldn't think for the longest time. I would work all day, come back at six when Sandi needed me, feed her, put her to bed and stay home. It was lonely at times but I didn't give much thought to men, certainly to remarriage. I'd worked hard to get my life in order. I didn't want any more change!

Then I met Harry. After a blind date, and a whirlwind courtship, we were married when Sandi was four. We took an extended honeymoon in Europe, then settled in a new city and new home.

It is important, I think, not to marry for the wrong reasons. In looking back, my attitude to this marriage was a big mistake. I was still carrying the load of guilt which I think all widows feel about the death of a husband. 'If I had done something more maybe I could have saved him.' I treated my second husband as if he were my first, catering to his every need. I spoiled him rotten. Harry wouldn't go to things I wanted to attend and because I was his wife I stayed home. For a very long time I said 'no' to things I felt I really wanted to do. It was fine then because I was having a great time being wife and mother for the second time around. Harry responded and loved my attention. I was hungry to be with Sandi. I was very happy at home and doing community volunteer work where I met many interesting and talented people and where I honed my own skills. On a volunteer basis, I conducted a Cantata when I was pregnant with my second daughter, Barb. I worked in a black choir gown which covered the works! I enjoyed that part of my life immensely. It was a great life and a great marriage — until the shoe got too tight.

Gradually, as the girls got into elementary school, I got back into my professional life teaching music privately, then at the Western Ontario Conservatory of Music. All these activities began to take me away from my husband more than in the past.

I didn't come to terms with my own needs until I got a severe personal jolt. First, Harry suffered a mild coronary after which he felt he needed more protecting. Then, one year after his heart attack, I did battle with cancer; eventually I had to have a radical mastectomy. The process of readjustment was very painful indeed. Through this period I found that Harry didn't really have a clue about my inner self and what I needed. There was only one person who really knew me and that was **me**. That's when I became very strong.

I began to take action. If I wanted to go somewhere, I would say, 'I'm going.' and I did go. I could go to a movie, to a dinner, anywhere by myself. I had just never thought my needs were that important before. At first my new direction threatened Harry. But that strength in me was a gift for both of us.

When Harry became terminally ill with cancer three years later, I became the nurse again. I was very, very tense because he was ill for a long time. Again, I had the support of friends and my daughters and their families were wonderful.

Interestingly, when I was widowed the second time, all my friends had suggestions for me. I must get a dog. I must sell my house. All sorts of things. And they meant well. All I needed was a dog to walk each night! And I love this house. The kids enjoy coming here and as long as I can afford to have someone help me inside and a gardener to help me outside, I'm going to stay in this house. I know what I need for myself. I simply did not listen to them.

Instead, I began to think about doing what I always wanted to do, to go on vacations, to travel. I was determined to do this and I have. Two years ago I decided to take the plunge and went with the Opera Guild to Vienna. I shared a room with an absolute stranger. We had a wonderful time. Last year I went with the same group to New York over the Christmas season. On New Year's Eve I was at the Met. having a ball.

My love is music. It keeps me young. We all have strong desires to do things — it may be to knit. Women need to listen to themselves. Find out their own solutions. Listen to themselves. That is the trick.

I am not lonely today. I have no desire to remarry. I enjoy being alone. I couldn't say that the first time I was widowed when I was much younger. The whole boy meets girl thing gets in the way when you are younger. Once I could get rid of that it was okay. I wouldn't want to have to ask my husband now if I could go to Halifax to adjudicate or whatever and when I got back to have sour grapes because I'd been away and he'd been neglected. I really like my freedom. I'm being very honest.

I know that some women feel they are only valuable if they are with a man. In this man's society they are meant to feel this way. And men perpetuate this myth. When we become widowed, we cling to the fact that we have made decisions as couples and done things as couples and we fear 'deciding' and 'doing' alone.

The most destructive emotion we have is fear. As a widow, I certainly became fearful. If fear comes up you just have to throw it off. It's like putting your toe in cold water and not being sure if you will go for a swim or if you would even enjoy getting wet. You just have to do it and find that the water's fine. In fact the swimming feels great!

Life for a widow changes drastically. The widow may not even see things the same way anymore. Friends will most likely change. Now my friends are with me because they like me and I them, not because of some connection with my husband.

As a widow, the second time, I feel that I can totally enjoy the fact that I am on my own. I can put the vase anywhere I like, go anywhere I want, with no judgment. As a widow, I have time. But that is not a burden to me because every day I find something to enjoy. To do that demands flexibility, something few of us claim within our marriages. Yesterday I had millions of things planned and then that gorgeous weather came along and it pulled at me and I had to get out. I enjoyed a walk and the sunshine and the blue sky. There are a lot of good things like that to enjoy in life — taking a walk, reading a good book, talking to a friend. You really don't need much more than that. Enjoy where you are today. Today is the day that really counts. Here I am at seventy-one years of age and still finding life exciting!

concluding comments

Sylvia was widowed twice. The first time she was very young, a single mother, concerned about supporting her child both emotionally and physically. She found her energies exhausted as a result of trying. She did have the support of fine *friends* who before Nat's death made the difficult tasks of caring for a baby and sick husband almost fun.

> Nice things happened. Friends were just marvelous. I think that's very important in life, to have that kind of support system.

Sylvia was a **hard worker** through this time, taking on full-time teaching at the Conservatory after Nat's death. She was also most **resourceful**, bartering her time as music director of a pre-school in exchange for her daughter's free enrolment. She took on a student who needed room and board to help with the child care. She did with less, just eleven dollars for the table one week, she recalled, and made fun for herself and Sandi at little cost. Sylvia knew her **priorities**, seemed to have boundless energy and a **positive attitude** which flowed with her as she lived her first widowhood experience.

Nevertheless, the role of widow even for Sylvia was exhausting and frightening. She began to doubt herself. Self-doubt fed self-doubt and, as Sylvia says, "My fear became almost a self-fulfilling prophesy. It was interfering with my teaching." What followed was remarkable given that it was the forties and Sylvia was young. Sylvia simply told herself to pull up her britches, cashed some of her carefully hoarded insurance savings and called a **psychiatrist for help**. Her ability to assess her situation and to seek help when she needed it, and to believe that she was worth the investment showed an incredible amount of **perspicacity**. Doubtless that move contributed to her knowing her own needs so well today.

After a second marriage, a second child, radical mastectomy and finally Harry's death, Sylvia moved into a second widowhood with a great deal of **self-confidence** and **determination**. She got lots of advice from friends. But she *listened to herself* and followed her own instincts:

> I must get a dog. I must sell my house. All sorts of things. They meant well. . . . I know what I need for myself. I simply did not listen to them.

Sylvia carried on after Harry's death in the pattern of doing what nurtured her, as she had found important in her marriage.

> Two years ago I went to Vienna. . . .last year I went. . . .to New York over the Christmas season. On New Year's Eve I was at the Met having a ball. My love is music. . . .Women need to listen to themselves. That is the trick.

Though Sylvia misses Harry who died eight years ago, she does not need a man in her life to be fulfilled, in fact admits to liking the freedom associated with being alone and being totally flexible. "I can put the vase anywhere I like, go anywhere I like with no judgement." She has a *positive attitude* toward the situation in which she finds herself today. She makes the best of it and possesses many resources to assist her in this. She is a *strong-willed, no-nonsense* woman. If fear comes up, you just "throw it off" she recommends. Remembering this process in her life she compares all her widowhood firsts (such as going to a movie, a dinner, a social event alone,) to going swimming:

> It's like putting your toe in cold water and not being sure if you will go for a swim or if you would enjoy getting wet. You just have to do it and find that the water's fine. In fact the swimming feels great!

Two years after our initial interview Sylvia remains a very active and productive woman. At the Western Ontario Conservatory of Music she teaches Piano and Pedagogy. She leads workshops for the Ontario Registered Music Teachers' Association throughout Ontario and examines students for the Western Conservatory. As an active member of the National Adjudication Association she travels across Canada to preside over music festivals from Vancouver Island to P.E.I. For those of her students and colleagues who aspire to teach well Sylvia is currently writing a book, *For the Love of Teaching*.

Sylvia's work and musical interests keep her busy. Despite her tight schedule she keeps in touch with very close friends and makes keeping actively involved with her four grandchildren, two little girls and two big boys an important priority. Her family is perhaps her greatest love. For Sylvia, the close relationship she has with her two daughters, that they are all three "on the same wave length," is her most treasured accomplishment.

I picture Sylvia sitting at her concert grand playing me a bit of Chopin as we conclude our interview together. I sense that I am with a truly remarkable woman who loves life! I believe part of this capacity comes from feeling pain and going beyond it without self-pity, to the place where she knows what she needs. Then she "goes for it." As Sylvia says:

> Enjoy where you are today. Today is the day that really counts. Here I am at seventy-one still finding life exciting!

7

Helen

a pool of men

beginning comments

I met Helen in 1987 through mutual friends. Aware that I was preparing to write a book about widows' experiences, she offered to share her story with me in order to help others. As we talked I marvelled at Helen's frank approach to many sensitive issues. Among the things we discussed were our vulnerability and sexuality. In the second category we covered everything from love affairs to re-marriage, with men friends, younger men, birth control, skin hunger and rejection in between. After our interview Helen and I lost touch for a few years until we began two years ago to work together with widowed women. In our discussions with them we faced the topic of sexuality head on. Amongst the participants we find that there is always a sense of relief when they discover, in a safe place, we can share just about anything!

Helen's experiences reiterate that widows have much in common. Unique to Helen's account is her ability to be particularly open about her own sexuality and how it changed and grew as she came to terms with the fact that she was a widow. Finding joy in living again parallelled her discovering the depth of her own sexuality for the first time.

HELEN

I met Robert when I was eighteen. I was shy, he self-assured and older. Our first date had to be approved by my mother, who liked him as soon as she met him! We dated for two years and were married one month before my twentieth birthday.

He was a nice man, had integrity and decency. Not perfect, Robert was also very impatient and determined, the latter a quality which would exert a positive influence in both of our lives after his first heart attack. Mostly, he was supportive of me and over the nineteen years of our marriage he encouraged me to pursue my university education. This I had to do sporadically as Robert began to need intermittent hospital care for chronic heart problems. After six years of marriage, we had our only child. The following year when Robert was young and I twenty-seven, he suffered a massive coronary from which he barely survived. After three weeks in intensive care, seven weeks in hospital and eight months off work, Robert was given little hope of ever working or playing again. The amazing thing was that he proved all the predictions wrong.

Determined to live life fully once again he began to walk to the mailbox every day. One year later he had worked up to jogging a mile daily. He went back to work, took up sailing and we carried on living a normal and active life! We did everything we wanted to do together over those years, travelled to many remote places. I always felt a small niggling fear about getting help if he needed it. But we did have twelve wonderful years together.

In the spring of 1983 he began to have severe and debilitating pain. His cardiologist found two of the major arteries to his heart blocked and strongly recommended coronary by-pass surgery. While we waited for a hospital bed his illness took control of our lives. He couldn't move. I did what I could, maintaining a job and family. During this hiatus period we talked a lot and it became clear that Robert feared being on a respirator after surgery. In the course of our conversations about this, Robert spoke about how he valued the quality and dignity of life. He would never want to be kept alive in a vegetative state. Talking about these things together at that time made it easier for me to make a difficult decision when the need arose later.

After a six month wait Robert had his by-pass operation, but it did not go well. The reasons were complex but basically, he was oxygen-deprived and suffered severe brain damage. He never regained consciousness. I sensed that something was wrong when he did not 'come to' in the recovery room but I was not told anything directly. Days passed and I began to feel panic when I couldn't seem to get any answers. Hospital residents avoided me; the surgeon himself never saw me after the operation. Finally, out of anger and frustration I demanded to be given some explanations. It was only then, two weeks after the operation, that a prognosis was shared with me. Robert would never regain consciousness, they said, would probably live a few months then die of some opportunistic infection. There was no future for him but life on a machine. It would not be what he wanted.

At last, understanding the situation, I met with the hospital's cardiac care director who repeated the earlier prognosis. As a result of our discussion I requested that life support systems be discontinued. I made this gut wrenching decision, traumatic as it was, alone. What calm I felt around my choice came from my absolute certainty that this would have been Robert's choice.

Though he couldn't have known I was with him, I didn't want Robert to die alone. I stayed with him over his last hour, held his hand, heard his breath settle slowly in his chest until it no longer supported a heart beat. He was dead. Seconds later a nurse came in and said, 'Are you finished yet?' Icy cold. I did not need her intrusion and impatience there but I had no experience about these matters. So I left. I found little patience or compassion in the hospital around my husband's death, a fact that fueled my anger later.

But it was fear, not anger, that dominated my life after Robert's death. Just before his operation, I had started a new job. I found returning to work a week after his death was the best thing for me. Working prevented my falling into the bottomless pit of my grief. At least for eight hours of each day I had to think about something other than Robert's death. Fellow workers were wonderful then, not expecting too much of me when I wasn't fully tracking. It was not until well into my second year of widowhood that I felt I began to take hold fully in my work. Before my husband's death, I believed myself to be a capable woman, really 'with it;' after, I was not at all sure of myself. Robert's death robbed me of all my self-confidence for a long time and made me fearful.

In this vulnerable state I needed everyone just to realize that I was having a bad time, to say, 'You're okay; whatever you do is fine.' I did not want criticism or advice. I needed them to be there for me, to listen and to approve. It is rare to have such nonjudgmental support. Luckily for me I had two very close women friends, one who had been recently divorced and one recently widowed, to help. They knew from personal experience what loss and aloneness really meant. They sensed when to call, what to say and when just to listen. I felt their love and understanding through the first critical year and a half, and without them I don't think I would have survived. These two women still remain my closest friends eight years and a marriage later!

Despite the steadfast support of friends and a fulfilling job I often felt overwhelmed by my situation. I was under incredible stress. Internally, I fought becoming the person I was having to become. I didn't want to deal with the house and the new job and family alone. I had to learn to say to myself, 'You can do it; you are capable.' Moreover, I felt dead for about a year. The numbness went all around me. At one point in this first year I realized I was messing up. I had the name of a therapist as a reference and, at that point, I went for help. He was a different resource from friends and family. He was a stranger and though it didn't come easily at first, eventually I could tell him anything. I could not do that always with family or close friends.

What he did that helped me most, I think, was to encourage me to express my anger. I was angry at doctors and nurses and neighbours and deserting friends; but mostly I was angry that Robert had died. Widows are expected to be hurt, sad, but never enraged. My therapist gave me permission to rage! He also informed me that these feelings were perfectly normal. Other widows felt them too. I was not alone or crazy. As I began to expend my anger I opened up new space. In time I would fill that open space with unexpected joy.

Going on a retreat the summer after Robert died gave me the opportunity to do some more grief work. I relived Robert's funeral as a celebration of his life here and interacted again with caring adults. I was beginning to feel the energy of life

returning to my body. I went home from my weekend interested
in being with people again. I began to accept invitations out
with friends which I had not been able to do before. As I became
more at ease about socializing I found myself wanting to get
to know other men. Of course, I didn't even know how to
converse easily after Robert. Our communicating was easy. I've
often thought that there should be a pool of men who would
escort widows just as friends, to ease them into the re-entry
stage of dating and mating again!

In the past my sexual experience had been limited to one
partner over a nineteen-year marriage. Our togetherness was
natural and relaxed. We enjoyed sex together and he knew what
pleasured me. It was a warm and intimate relationship. When
Robert was gone I felt a terrible loneliness. Then, as I came
out of the shock I became curious about what it would be like
to have an affair with another man. I needed someone to talk
to about this too. Sharing sexual feelings and 'secrets' was
difficult even with the therapist I by now trusted.

At first it was like going to a dentist. My jaw was clenched.
I did not want to speak. But I learned to do so and together
we discussed the fear and guilt I felt around getting involved
with other men and being a sexual woman again.

I felt guilty and confused about my physical needs. I needed
hugs. I can't think of a time I needed warm arms to hold me
more than after Robert's death. There is such a feeling of letting
go when we are held. I didn't even know I needed holding until
I got the need met. I found a way to satisfy this craving non-
sexually at first. I could get hugs from special women friends.
I could hug my cat, anything with warmth and vitality to share
was huggable and helpful. I also needed to be touched; I know
this now as skin hunger. Without it old people die and babies
don't progress as they should. In terms of touching my own
body, I felt a tremendous amount of guilt. Pleasuring myself
is not something that was approved in my upbringing. I felt
I shouldn't be doing this. However, I found that I could accept
it as a viable way to meet my sexual needs at a time when
I was without a partner.

Then, when I felt ready to be with another man and the opportunity presented itself, I was ready to be totally involved in the love-making process. I did discover some unexpected problems in my first physical union after Robert. Despite my own desire, fear almost made me say 'no.' The thought of taking my clothes off in front of another man, revealing all the lumps and bumps and sags was horrifying. When you're in a marriage you don't even think about all these things! Then there was guilt. Guilt almost dissuaded the desire. I felt torn. I wanted to love and be loved. But by making love with someone else I was acknowledging that I was alive and Robert was not. I was recognizing his absence with my whole physical being, not just my head. A whole raft of emotions surged through me. 'Touch me, but don't touch me,' went through my head. I was depressed and happy. I cried and I felt deep passion. Needless to say my new partner was a little perplexed.

I also remember vividly the intensity of this first sexual experience after Robert's death. I think much of the high came from the joy I was feeling about being alive. I still had a physical body and I could still enjoy a physical life. Essentially sexual expression is an expression of life. Because I was coming to life after a long period of numbness, this event was something to celebrate.

Around me while I was joyfully exploring my own sexuality, there was little celebration. When I started dating, my family disapproved. The neighbourhood in which Robert and I had lived for fifteen years seemed particularly judgmental. I could have hand written scarlet letters across my forehead and the neighbours would have said, 'right.' I expect they felt that I was just being 'the merry widow,' that I was not being true to Robert. That was it! I was expected to be true to him for the rest of my life. A bit like committing Hindu 'suttee' where the widow dies on the funeral pyre of her dead husband. I was just beginning to feel alive again. My life was **not** over.

I made an important decision for myself then. Realizing that the old suburban environment did not nurture me, I made plans to relocate in the country which I loved. There, I could be myself.

I loved my new found ability to come and go freely, to be anonymous, to fully welcome new experiences. That move was the best thing I did!

Another new risk I took centred around getting seriously involved in a relationship with a man fourteen years younger than I. The physical pull between us was incredible and the love-making terrific. I was really revelling in the sex. For the first time in my life I was taking the responsibility for my own pleasure without the burden of guilt. By this time I had learned to accept the fact that Robert was dead and I was alive and than neither of us had any choice in that. I gave myself permission to enjoy my life while I had it. In allowing myself this relationship, I was doing just that!

Some problems developed in this relationship, too. The first was quite funny. I was concerned about the fact that I could still get pregnant (Robert had had a vasectomy). I knew that I had to take responsibility for my sexuality and decided to have a tubal ligation. My doctor referred me to a gynecologist who, in the course of the pre-op examination, asked about my marital status. When I said, 'widow,' he literally jumped, shock written all over his face. 'What are you doing this for?' Widows are not expected to be sexual beings! Despite the doctor's obvious malaise, I had the operation.

What happened next is very funny, but only in retrospect. The very day of my tubal when I returned home from the hospital, the young man called me to say that he was terribly sorry, but there was someone else. My initial reaction was, 'You ----.' I was devastated. How could the relationship be great one minute then 'I don't want you' the next? How could I accept this decision? It took me a long, long time just to pick myself up and go on with life. In retrospect I can say honestly that learning to accept rejection and go on again to live and enjoy was a very important lesson for me.

I learned and I grew. I was getting to know about risking and to become more comfortable with it in many areas of my life. Risking was like putting one foot over a precipice: it involved danger. But maybe there would be something very wonderful over that precipice that I would not want to miss. When I considered my options, sitting safe at home for the rest of my life was not what I wanted. I decided to take the risks. My choice was to live fully.

As opportunities arose I became involved in other relationships with men, some sexual. There were three men in my life before I met my present husband. I learned from each one of them. I found that it was important not to become so dependent on a man that I couldn't function without him. Even now that I am married I remind myself that I worked hard to get to the place where I could rely on myself. I don't want to give up that ability. I was okay before my new marriage and I will be unhappy if something were to happen in this relationship, too. But I have the resources to survive. Knowing that is a power that I value highly.

I am aware that I have grown as a woman through my experiences after the death of my husband. Robert's death has given me insight into so many things. Certainly, I know more about myself and my sexuality. Now I know what I want. I have changed in many ways. If Robert could come back to visit me now, just for a few minutes, I think he would respect and value the woman that his death has helped me become!

concluding comments

Helen lost her husband suddenly when she was thirty-nine and had a new job and a growing child to challenge her. She was under considerable stress. At first her two greatest resources were her *work* and her *friends*. At work being occupied eight hours a day at tasks which kept her interest and attention, prevented her from sinking "into the bottomless pit of my grief." Work was an asset for Helen. Friends were an additional boost. Work friends treated her well and helped fill in when she wasn't tracking. In addition, two very close friends gave her a special kind of support because they had "been there" before her. These women friends, one recently widowed, one divorced, were non-judgmental, just what Helen needed in her vulnerable state, friends who could say, "You're okay; whatever you do is fine."

Then at a time when even work and friends were not enough, when she felt she was really messing up, Helen knew where to find *professional help* and did not hesitate to seek it for herself. Only with a family therapist was she able to *get out the feelings*, deep anger and guilt, which were present and counterproductive in her life. As she says:

> Widows are expected to be hurt, sad but never enraged. My therapist gave me permission to *be angry*.

There was more *grief work* to do for Helen. In a *retreat* setting Helen re-enacted Robert's funeral as a celebration of his life. Somehow that validated his existence and energized Helen to take up her own life more fully. With the energy that comes from finding heartfelt support from others for one's self-discovery and growth, Helen returned home and began to live in a new way. She started to care how she looked, began to *socialize* and to *enjoy life* just a little more. When she realized that her current environment did not nurture her, she moved. She became *decisive*, aware of her own needs, and *courageous*. A move to the country parallelled a move into exploring new relationships, into exploring her own sexuality and into living life more fully. *Curiosity* was another asset and resource for Helen. What kind of life do I really want to lead? What are other men like? She set out to discover answers for herself. One such quest led her to meet a new man who would become her husband.

Helen also learned by *risking*, learned through her pain. She realized her pain as part of growth, as the price sometimes exacted for feeling the highs of life so intensely:

> I remember. . . .the intensity of this first sexual experience after Robert's death. . . .I was coming to life after a long period of numbness. . . .His death has given me insight into so many things.

Helen comments that one of the most important learnings for her in all of these last eight years has been that she is a *survivor.*

> Regardless of what happens to me, I can survive. House, money, trips, responsibilities, cars, business: I handled it all. Remembering installing a dimmer switch in the dining room, turning it on, having it WORK. I had a tremendous satisfaction in that.

She knows that she can rely on herself. It is a powerful resource to know that one will always be there for oneself. Being strong, acknowledging that strength, and putting things in place to ensure that one maintains that power is an important life skill. Helen learned through her widowhood that she can do it all.

8

Peggy

once more to dance

I was empty after Bob died. I didn't know who I was on my own and, therefore, I felt valueless. Filling the emptiness left by my husband's death meant finding my inner core much like an archaeologist on a dig, unearthing bit by bit, polishing it and recognizing it as a part of myself.

I found discovering who I was a challenge. It meant, firstly, listening to myself and excluding the inner voices that were not truly valid to me. For example I had always been a perfectionist. I possessed a strong inner voice which judged me harshly expecting more and more. During the first years of widowhood I had to be the perfect mother and father, never ask for help and so on. When a crisis with the children arose after Bob's death, the judge in me said, "go it alone" until another part of me, small and very weak at first, had compassion and urged me to do something. That was the voice from my centre. It talked me into seeking help. This was a hard step to take. The old way was to refuse outside help. We were a family who kept its troubles to itself. The pull between what I needed and what was acceptable was great. More out of desperation than courage, I chose to take a new path, to get further into my own healing.

There were fears unleashed as I began to free myself. Fears about changing my way of living, about what people would think, about the cost of it all in terms of time and effort. But when I realized what was really important to me I began to feel that I had no choice.

I began to change. A new home and new work were risks that I took to satisfy the new inner voice that I was acknowledging for the first time in my life. I also began to write this book.

"To write is to stand in judgment of yourself," says author Robertson Davies. To write, I think, is also to know oneself. An unrelenting task, yes. In fact, there can be no more important education anywhere than that which puts one in touch with one's very essence. Through my writing I have found myself. And through the grace of my friends, I have learned to love myself. That, too was a challenge! As woman alone I began to interact more honestly and openly with the people I met. I found that being more truly myself drew new friends to me, solidified old friendships and lost me the rest. There are no regrets in this. It was encouraging to be living, and speaking, and writing from my core. My "be-ing" was validated both through my self-love and through the love of others.

During this time I was constantly on the search for what I valued, what I found nurturing in order to flesh out my new identity. I had to find my own "bliss list," as Jennifer James calls it, then remember it and live it. Seven years after Bob's death I wrote from my core this personal list.

Toward fulfillment I:

allow myself time for myself
gaze at something or someone I love
allow myself to be loving and to love
learn to hear my own still small voice
put myself first
learn to love myself
love my children, my enemies and my parents as myself
learn compassion
change my mind
take risks
live without fear
try new things
dare to be different
hug a tree
garden
plant a seed
sing a song
listen to music
do yoga
meditate
be a good friend
decide what is really important to me
chop out the unimportant things, associates
slow down

play
be curious
read a lot
ask questions
speak my own mind
trust that all will be well
dance more
watch a bird
get up to see the sun rise over a lake
see the moon set
make love on a beach
accept depression and pain as teachers and temporary
don't fight intuition
trust one's elf (oneself)
open up with others
really listen to the people in my life
don't try to manipulate or control
buy less
travel light with arms and legs free to swing along
don't fret the small stuff
remember 'we've been through worse, Peg'
see every part of our living as learning
trust that there is life after death
do not fear
dare
love
watch squirrels play in the tree tops
find quiet space for myself
accept and rejoice in solitude
value the times I communicate well with another being
enjoy the ordinary
risk
don't ever fake it
let go of what others think
speak from the place of deep knowing
dream, then make it happen
listen to my subconscious

get in touch with my personal spirituality
do not fear despair; desperation forces action
keep a dream log
interpret my dreams with help if necessary

Eight years ago I felt no joy in my life; now I feel it often and deeply. I am not empty anymore. I like my life and I like the people in it, including myself. I do not live by my "bliss list" every day though I would like to. I still get depressed, hurt, angry, irrational, jealous. I am the same old Peg. But I also know that I am larger than my emotions. I am capable of directing my life.

Discovering that my life has meaning and value has taken time and work, work for which Bob's death was the catalyst, my self-discovery the reward. Now each day is a mystery, a special event, a challenge, a blessing. I will never be tomorrow just what I am today because each day has a lesson for me and each day I grow. I would not have it any other way.

I just took a writing break, walked into my kitchen, pulled out a frosted glass for ice tea, dropped it upside down on the kitchen floor so that the sugared rim stuck to the dust underfoot, and cursed myself thinking

> You are the dumbest, biggest klutz around. How can you possibly write all that crap about personal fulfillment when you can't even handle a glass without dropping it?

Well, there I am folks and that is my life. The dumb and the profound living side by side in me. I am real and so are you and so is our time on this earth. Worse things could happen than dropping my glass on my perpetually dirty kitchen floor. Worse things could happen than seeing my fallibilities.

It would be worse, I think, to live forever unseen, never "to be" for oneself. The worst, I believe.

If you are reading this book front to back you have met many parts of me. If you are a widow and you have made comparisons, you will know that my personal reality may not be the same as yours. I suspect, just like the millions of stones upon the beach where miraculously no two are the same, widowed women differ in at least one way — perhaps in many. It is comforting to know that each of us is unique.

It is also comforting somewhere in the process of healing after the death of our husbands to know that widows share stages and emotions. We share the stages of grief: shock, denial, acceptance and growth. We all feel guilt, sadness, anger, helplessness, longing and despair at some time or other during our healing process.

But sometimes we forget that we all share more than hurdles and hurting. We share wonderful accomplishments and new growth. As widowed women all of us have been courageous, capable, resourceful, independent, inventive, feisty. Many of us become new women doing things we've never dreamed of doing before. Do we appreciate our strengths? Do we celebrate our transformations? It is time after the death of our husbands to celebrate ourselves. Once more, it is time to dance!

Afterword

It is Labour Day, 1992. I have been virtually deserted. Two of my children have flown west to school and the two "at-home" kids are visiting with friends, leaving me to enjoy a gloriously empty house and an hour of solitude. I love this alone time. For me it is a time to reconnect with myself. So I sit in the quiet of this late summer afternoon ready to review the past year.

It has been a good year: probably about the best I could have wished for because, in its course, I have realized a passionate dream — to write a book. When I set out to write *Wife After Death* I did not know how to make this dream a reality. What I did know was that I had a compulsion to share the wisdom about loss and transformation that I'd found through experiencing my husband's death and the grief following it.

Writing the book was both exhilarating and difficult. Through it I met many wonderful people and did a lot of my own grief work. With writing the book there were also unexpected challenges. It took a lot of time, energy and commitment to research and create *Wife After Death*. And that was, as I would discover, only the beginning. Getting a book published and distributed was next and I knew nothing about either process. Several times I put the project on hold because I'd lost faith in it.

"Maybe I'm just doing my own therapy," I thought.

No question, self doubt was an enemy to my dream! I encountered several more tangible interruptions. I sent my manuscript to a Toronto publisher by registered mail but it was "misplaced". Canada Post was not helpful. I caught the "constant rejection" plague. Again and again I heard from prospective publishers that someone else would probably be the very one to publish my work, but as for them, "No thank you." Further, said many, "Death doesn't sell."

"What about life?" I thought. "Don't they know that death is a part of life? This book is about LIFE."

Looking back, their rejections should not have surprised me. I was learning for the second time what I'd discovered immediately after Bob's death. We live in a death-denying society. The publishing industry simply reflected the larger community's denial of death.

Now, I believe the delays I encountered were valuable because they gave me time to facilitate my own healing. Otherwise, I might not have had the insight necessary to complete *Wife After Death*.

Little things helped me stay committed to my dream when all else seemed to be going wrong. Often, as I worked on *Wife After Death* I met widows for whom the women's stories I'd collected seemed tailor-made. To them I loaned a rough draft, a chapter here, another there. For some, those chapters were a lifeline. Knowing this helped me to continue.

In January 1991, five years after beginning *Wife After Death* I concluded it was "now or never". I decided to invest in my dream and become my own publisher. Magically, things began to happen. As Goethe once said:

> There is one elementary truth, the ignorance of which kills countless ideas and splendid plans: the moment one definitely commits oneself, then Providence moves too. All sorts of things occur to help one that never otherwise would have occurred ...
> Whatever you can do,
> Or dream you can do,
> Begin it.
> Boldness has genius, power and magic in it.
> Begin it now.

With renewed energy I searched out other self-published authors, found them willing to share secrets with me about the publishing process, read the "how to" books, took out a small loan and applied for an ISBN number. While finishing a university course and doing private grief counselling in London, I organized the final writing, picture taking, editing, typesetting, planning and cover design for *Wife After Death*. It was an exhilarating time!

After months of rewrites, edits, checks and double-checks, I mailed the so-called vandykes (final book before printing) to my printer and waited. Unexpectedly and before deadline, two heavy cardboard book boxes arrived at my front door. No one was home to share this moment with me, but I can tell you it was a moving experience. Seeing the book for the first time after its six-year gestation period I felt like the new parent. As I held "my baby" in my hand, I was both proud and protective. For a short time, I was reluctant to put this vulnerable part of myself out into the world. But I had written it for others. So out it went, first to a conference on "Children and Death" at Kings' College at the University of Western Ontario where I was conducting a workshop, then to friends, clients and bookstores in southwestern Ontario. Local newspapers wrote about the book and it began to sell. More important for me than all the sales (though I liked those!) was the feedback from readers. They confirmed that the book had value:

> Your book is marvellous. I couldn't put it down. The stories are so beautifully told. They go way beyond how to (as in grieving and recovery). The women tell us much about ourselves.

> As a child of one of your widows, could I suggest that you ensure the book is given to their children, at the time that everything is happening? I would have found it tremendously reassuring to know why my mother was being unpredictable and incapable ... and that such behaviour is normal!

> I was very impressed by the coping done by such a diverse group. Each of the stories leave a lasting impression of women who have not only survived their tragic circumstances but have triumphed over them. Thank you for your very moving and helpful book.

In January 1992, Fitzhenry & Whiteside who had also seen and liked the book, decided to help me with its distribution. Together we began to publicize and sell *Wife After Death* across Canada. I agreed to a promotion tour out west where I was able to connect with my two children who were at the University of British Columbia, in addition to participating in several radio shows, a live phone-in spot and a T.V. feature. New stuff for me. But I had a "wonder full" time. The trip challenged me in many ways as my journal notes show here:

* * *

London, April 26

In bed at 11:45. Up at 5:20 tomorrow to shower for the trip. Right now I am tired and feel lonely. In a way, I don't want to leave home. I realize how important my familiar territory is.

Calgary, April 27

Excellent flights from London to Toronto and Toronto to Calgary. Interviews arranged by Donna Tai at Fitzhenry & Whiteside were good. #1 The telephone interview with Kevin Usselman (newly married, not read book) . #2 Paul Baumberg 3/4 of an hour. Excellent. Got in touch with different issues. #3 CBC Radio "Homestretch" Jeff Collins. Excellent. Read book. Interested in my story and the mechanics of my grief work i.e., psychodrama (reliving the events of the past through dramatization) and journaling. Went with F&W's rep., Penny, to "4th Street Rose" for lunch. Nice. I'm needing to eat light during this time. If I feel heavy, I don't think clearly. Doing interviews demands lucidity. Now at 1:30 p.m. I'm feeling really zapped — totally. I need a sleep.

In air, April 28

Air Canada Flight 225 to Vancouver where I plan to see my children, Cathy and Matt. My friend in Calgary, Lyn, mentioned how hard it is to look at baby pictures of her children, Tim, Paul, Joe, Mark and Beth. I know how she feels. They grow up so quickly. I think about Sarah and Jeff at home and Matt and Cathy here.

I still picture them in their entirety — from infancy to present. To me they are not 15, 21, 23, 25, but every age and stage they've weathered. Still my babies, but bigger!

Re interviews to-day: Interesting though difficult in that you meet, connect, then disconnect, with a little dose of discovery in there somehow, all in the space of 20-45 minutes. I had no trouble being grounded. Maybe I was a little wordy? I forgot to guard against "ums" and "you knows". Went into the subject matter totally. I'm tired. I'm glad I'll have tomorrow off and glad I'll be getting more regular sleep!! Must go wash hands before landing.

Vancouver, April 29
Free day. Moved Cathy out of her apartment and us into a great Bed and Breakfast.

Vancouver, April 30
11:00 a.m. to radio station LG 73 with Stone Phillips, in Bermuda shorts. Before we start I ask him (and every other interviewer I've met on this trip) if he's had a personal loss recently. In this case "yes" was the answer. I want to know if there's active grief going on here; the interviewer also needs to know that this book, ostensibly about others, is about him/herself as well. Grief links us all.

2:00 met CJVB AM's Richard Weichsler. Multi-language station. Deep and impressive interview.

1:15 p.m. CFUN with Dave.

2:00 p.m. met Cathy Tate for a Lifestyles interview for newspaper, *The Province*. In their cafeteria enjoying a panoramic view of mountains and city, we talked over cups of scalding tea. Difficult to focus on loss and death in the presence of such incredible splendour!

Vancouver, May 1
Began to-day rushing to Matt's for a telephone interview from Calgary and having no call come through. Annoying — what to do?

Interview with Julie Brown CKIS FM. Interesting. Felt less at home with her than men interviewers. A surprise for me. She had read most of my book and knew what to ask. Her last question was loaded: "What is your main message for the world?" I did not hesitate. "Live life fully," I replied. Should have said "If widowed don't be afraid to ask for help."

No, Peg. Stay with the gut response.

After the interview Cath and I went to the Queen Elizabeth and the Van Dusen Gardens, both of which were magnificent. Then dinner with Matt and Cath overlooking English Bay. Cost a fortune. Took Matt to his apartment and home early. I am writing now in bed.

Thoughts about the trip:

I miss Bob.

I like doing the interviews.

Some interviewers stick more than others.

All the interviewers are melting togehter.

I'm tired. — It's tiring. — My brain is down. — Kids are great. — Scenery beautiful. I've walked in it but not been part of it. I'm distracted getting into and coming down off my ''work''. And it is work, returning to the past and events in my book with readers and radio personalities. Wish I'd written a funny book. The trip could have been a little lighter.

All's well. Thinking of all my loved ones and in particular, Bob.

Victoria, May 2, 3

Weekend ''off''. Sat. a.m. all three of us set out for Tsawwassen and the ferry to Vancouver Island. Drove into Victoria and staked out a great B&B. Shopped till we dropped, enjoyed Butchart Gardens; found a pub where we sampled B.C. brew and watched a hockey game. Beautiful place, friendly people.

Victoria, May 4

Back to work. Getting ready for my first live talk show with Joe Easingwood CFAX and am more nervous than ever. I've already heard Joe mention on air, as I sit waiting my turn, Sally Armstrong and David Suzuki, who will precede and follow me. Panic. Who am I in all this? I'd like to have all the women in the book and my women's group and my kids here for support. I invoke their presence. Who am I kidding? I'm doing this alone.

On to CKDA 1200 & CFMS 98.5. Monday afternoon on the last leg of this tour. It's had its ups and downs. Excitement and travel the up side; exhaustion the down.

I realize what a poor businesswoman I am. — Have not been

keeping all my receipts! — Also have felt a bit rushed and even muddled at times.

Sooke Harbour, Vancouver Island, May 5
A bit of R and R after the tour. Sitting on the porch at Sooke Harbour House, Whiffen Spit Road. Arrived here about 4:30 and walked the spit. Picked up seashells and a yin/yang stone. Smell of seashells and seaweed strong and beautiful. As I sit on the deck here the view is spectacular. Directly in front are pink- and orange-filled window boxes. Beyond, the trim gardens and the sea — low tide — so much of pebbles and stones and sea-weed. The ocean itself calm and cool as glass and a peninsula of land fingering out into the placid water. Then, across the Strait, the white-capped Olympic Mountains shrouded two thirds up in mist. The sun is shining warm on my head and it is one glori-ous day!

Sooke, May 6   Early a.m.
Dinner last night:
Cathy: Vegetarian sorrels in buckwheat crepes; Matt: honey-glazed breast of chicken
Peg: Pacific rockfish and fresh spot prawns. Sauce of fennel and carrots.
Dessert: Honey and apricot, blueberry and apple, and raspberry and rose geranium sorbet.
Lovely.
Time to get up.
Saw more of the island to-day. Beaches are "super natural", forests grand. Then, a jarring clearcut slash on a mountain face shocks us all. This feels like death of another kind. There is grief here too.
Return to Vancouver tomorrow.

Over Vancouver, May 7
Just airborne — up safely, though it feels a bit rocky at the moment. I left Cathy at one part of the airport and Matt in Van-couver. I really don't like that — separation — though I know it's normal, natural and healthy: like many other painful things in life.

121

It's been a great couple of weeks. The work was fascinating though it has a dreamlike quality, unreal now, especially since I won't likely ever hear or see the results of my interviews. It's odd (awed) to be in close quarters with another human being for 10-20 minutes to discuss soul-sized subjects, to connect in some way, then to move on as if the connection had never been made.

What this teaches me about myself is that I like more intimate connections, more lasting moments, deeper friendships. We can validate our own selves only to a point. Eventually, inevitably, our very being demands validation by others — if only for an instant.

This trip has taught me many things. Blessed be.

*   *   *

The spring book tour was a success in every way. Over the summer, sales of *Wife After Death* continued and by fall we were aware that we should consider preparing and perhaps running a second edition. So it has been a "very good year", one which I will not easily forget!

I have learned much from following my heart into a project which touched my life so deeply. I have learned that it is possible to dream and to make that dream come true. I've learned to listen to my own intuitive voice as I make important choices in my life. I've learned that people are very much alike and good and true, if given the love and support they deserve. I've learned to trust again and to be willing to take risks. I've also learned about my negative self. I am a hard taskmaster and a critical judge. Over much of this year I've caught myself thinking "but I could do more, the book could do better." I've had trouble celebrating my accomplishments or seeing myself as a success. I'd like to change that part of myself and allow for more celebration and fun in my life!

Next month will be the tenth anniversary of my husband's death. "Seven years a widow," my son, Matt, shot out at me a few years ago when I was complaining of feeling burned out with others' grief. "Isn't it enough?" he challenged. Not until now have I been able to admit the wisdom in his challenge.

For the first few years after Bob's death, I denied my widow-hood. Then as I began to do my grief work, I realized that "widow" was my reality and gradually over time I was able to accept, even say and write, that I was not "wife" anymore, but "widow".

Accepting that new identity was an important part of my personal grief work. Accepting the widow within myself then taking her out to meet others both personally and professionally has been crucial to my coming to terms with my new self after loss. But I sense a subtle change in me. More and more I feel distanced, separate from the "widow place" both internally and externally. This distance is not the same denial I lived in my first years of widowhood. It is something altogether different. The distance is evidence of a shift within me. To deny what you are inhibits growth; to know what you are, accept it, then move on, facilitates growth. The personal shift I feel is evidence of a new growth. I have come full circle. "Widow" no longer fits. That label diminishes me now, makes me live something which I am not and stifles my growing into all I may be.

The message is clear. I believe I have done my grief work. I do not have to remember the past out of guilt. I have nothing to be guilty about. I do not have to remember the past in order to keep Bob alive. He lives in our children. He will be present in the milestones of their lives, when each graduates, when each marries, when grandchildren are born. And he lives in me. He lives in the unexpected moment, when I glimpse his face in an old photo album, when I smell hyacinths in the spring air and when I hear autumn winds rustle leaves on a crisp Algonquin day. Bob is dead, but he has not left me!

I have nothing to lose by turning the corner and leaving the widow behind. What holds me back? Compassion, dependency and fear. Compassion for the widow I was. Dependency on what I know, what is comfortable. And fear. Fear of change. Fear of the new. If I choose change, I will again be setting out on uncharted waters, leaving the safe and the known. But my choice is to set a new course, despite my fear, to celebrate that choice and risk moving ahead into the unknown.

Before beginning this new journey I want to acknowledge a mentor who has taught me so many things over the last ten years. This mentor came uninvited into my life. He was not welcome and he was not my friend. But it was his presence that forced me to take up my own life and live my own dreams. My mentor is Death.

It is an incredible irony that Death, once my greatest enemy, has become my greatest teacher. Without his presence I would have continued to live an unexamined and unconscious life. Without him I could never have experienced the depths of my sorrow or known the peaks of my joy. With him as teacher I have learned that life does have meaning and that love can conquer fear.

Death has given me the precious gift of Life.

Life

Some people
Plod
Like the old milk-wagon nag
Reined and blinkered
Through their world.

I refuse to be
A milk horse
On the route of life.

I will run my course
As a proud mare
   Head held high
      Ears pricked
         Nostrils flaring
            Eyes wide open

Galloping

Bold

Free

Into the wind

Feeling each rut
with blood
and bones
and heart
And soul

Unprotected from pain
Vulnerable in passion
Risking it all.

So when I, at last
Cross the finish line
I will have
No doubt
That I have been
A L I V E !

Bibliography

Books mentioned in *Wife After Death*

Caine, Lynn. *Being a Widow*. Boston: K. G. Hall, 1990.

Caine, Lynn. *Lifelines*. Garden City: Doubleday, 1978.

Grollman, Earl. *Talking About Death*. Boston: Beacon Press, 1970.

Grollman, Earl. *What Helped Me When My Loved One Died*. Boston: Beacon Press, 1981.

Hinton, John. *Dying*. Middlesex: Penguin Books, 1972.

James, Jennifer. *Success Is the Quality & Your Journey* (expanded edition). New York: Newmarket, 1986.

Kubler-Ross, Elisabeth. *Children and Death*. New York: Collier, 1983.

Kubler-Ross, Elisabeth. *Living With Death and Dying*. New York: Collier, 1981.

Kubler-Ross, Elisabeth. *On Death and Dying*. New York: Collier, 1969.

Kushner, Harold S. *When Bad Things Happen to Good People*. New York: Avon, 1981.

Krementz, Jill. *How It Feels When a Parent Dies*. New York: Knopf, 1988.

LeShan, Eda. *Learning to Say Goodby*. New York: Avon, 1976.

Lewis, C. S. *A Grief Observed*. New York: Bantam, 1963.

Lewis, C. S. The *Problem of Pain*. Glasgow: Collins, 1940.

Moody, Raymond. *Life After Life*. New York: Bantam, 1975.

Westberg, Granger, E. *Good Grief: a Constructive Approach to the Problems of Loss*. Philadelphia: Fortress, 1971.

Wylie, Betty Jane. *Beginnings: a book for widows*. Toronto: McLelland and Stewart, 1977.